MW00417143

The Way It Was and Other Writings

 Jesús Colón

Edited with an Introductory Essay
by Edna Acosta-Belén and Virginia Sánchez Korrol

Arte Público Press
Houston
Texas
1993

This book is made possible through support from the Rockefeller Foundation, the National Endowment for the Arts (a federal agency), the Lila Wallace-Reader's Digest Fund and the Andrew W. Mellon Foundation.

Arte Público Press
University of Houston
Houston, Texas 77204-2090

Cover design by Mark Piñón

Colón, Jesús, 1901–1974
    The way it was, and other writings : historical vignettes about the New York Puerto Rican community / by Jesús Colón : edited with and introductory essay by Edna Acosta-Belén and Virginia Sánchez Korrol.
        p.   cm.
    Includes bibliographical references.
    ISBN 1-55885-057-0 : $12.00
    1. Puerto Ricans—New York (N.Y.) 2. New York (N.Y.)—Social life and customs. 3. Colón, Jesús, 1901–1974. I. Acosta-Belén, Edna. II. Sánchez Korrol, Virginia. III. Title.
F128.9.P85C65   1993
305.868'729507471—dc20   92-42443

                                                                CIP

The paper used in this publication meets the requirements of the American National Standard for Permanence of Paper for Printed Library Materials Z39.48-1984. ∞

Copyright © 1993 by Center for Puerto Rican Studies,
Hunter College, CUNY
Printed in the United States of America

This book is dedicated to:

Chris Bose, for her commitment to share and learn about the Puerto Rican spirit.

Doña Elisa Santiago de Baeza, who nurtured a deep appreciation for family and community in all her children.

Contents

Preface 7

The World of Jesús Colón
Edna Acosta-Belén and *Virginia Sánchez Korrol* 13

Part I: *The Way It Was*

Castor Oil: Simple or Compound 33

Jesús Is Graduating Tonight 37

The Silent Contest 39

The Head on the Statue of Liberty 41

Nice to Have Friends in All Walks of Life 42

A Bright Child Asks a Question 46

He Couldn't Guess My Name 47

Dalmau 49

Angels in My Hometown Church 53

The Meanest Man in My Hometown 55

The *Fanguito* Is Still There 57

Part II: Other Writings

The Two United States 61

The Jewish People and Us 65

My Wife Does Not Work 67

Bitter Sugar: Why Puerto Ricans Leave Home 69

Pilgrimage of Prayer 74

Phrase Heard on a Bus 77

Little Rock 80

A Growing Minority 84

Colonial Showplace 86

The Meaning of Algebra 88

The Negro in Puerto Rican History 90

The Negro in Puerto Rico Today 93

Puerto Rican Migrant Labor 96

Arthur Schomburg and Negro History 98

Statement by Jesús Colón to the Walter Committee
     on Un-American Activities 100

Appendices

Biographical Chronology 103

Bibliography of Jesús Colón's Writings 105

List of Photographs 125

About the Editors 127

Preface

In preparing this anthology of a handful of the many essays that Jesús Colón planned to include in his "The Way It Was," which remained unfinished and unpublished, we are attempting to introduce readers to an unknown body of writings by one of the most important figures of the early years of the New York Puerto Rican community. Colón's death in 1974 came as an irreparable loss to the community, but his legacy remains in the extensive library and collection of papers which were donated by his estate and the Communist Party of America to the Centro de Estudios Puertorriqueños at Hunter College. The Jesús Colón Papers Collection at the Centro Library includes many of the journalist's published and unpublished writings as well as a wide array of invaluable documents that chronicle the evolution of the Puerto Rican community during the first half of the twentieth century. Recognizing the importance of documenting how the New York Puerto Rican community evolved, Colón proved to be an avid collector of articles, newsletters, leaflets, newspaper and magazine clippings, reports, photographs and personal correspondence that give testimony to his extraordinary life and active participation in the social, political and cultural life of the migrant community. He was also a prolific journalist and his writings, together with those above mentioned materials that he so meticulously collected, attest to his visionary role in anticipating the importance of preserving a historical record of the building of the New York Puerto Rican community for the future generations.

Among The Jesús Colón Papers at the Centro Library there are several versions of an outline for a forthcoming book with the working title "The Way It Was: Puerto Ricans from Way Back." This manuscript, which Colón was unable to complete during his life, was intended to be a compilation of many of the essays or sketches, as he preferred to call them, that the author had published throughout his long journalistic career and of new material he had already finished or was planning to write specifically for the book. It is evident from examining the titles and descriptions of the sketches listed in the book outlines that a large number came from Colón's newspaper columns written during five decades. He lists more than 250 essay items in his last version of the outline. However, among his papers there are only eleven drafts of texts which are identified and selected for inclusion in "The Way It Was." All of these sketches are included in Part I of this anthology.

The reality of dealing with an incomplete manuscript for "The Way It Was" confronted the editors with the problem of providing a sense of coherence to this anthology while remaining faithful to Colón's original conception of his unfinished manuscript. Mindful of these goals, we went back to his first and only other book, *A Puerto Rican in New York and Other Sketches*, published in 1961, and compared its content and structure to the book outlines the author prepared for "The Way It Was." We came to the conclusion that Colón had planned and organized "The Way It Was" along similar lines as *A Puerto Rican in New York*. As with the first, the new book was also to include a series of anecdotal accounts of the Puerto Rican migrant experience and of the daily lives and survival struggles of ordinary people from his perspective as community activist and participant in the many cultural, social and political organizations that emerged during his more than half century of living in New York City. In "The Way It Was," Colón also was planning to include biographical profiles of important Puerto Rican community figures of his time. The main difference between these two books was that "The Way It Was" was intended to be a more encompassing and detailed historical account of the early Puerto Rican community, one that perhaps would fill in some of the historical gaps and consider other important issues and personalities that had been left out of a *A Puerto Rican in New York*.

With all of these considerations in mind, the editors selected for Part II of this anthology several pieces from the large body of Colón's published and unpublished essays which best complemented the writings he left prepared for "The Way It Was" included in Part I. Most of these other writings take us a step further in capturing Colón's view of his surrounding world. We have chosen those sketches that best represent the concerns and themes that he continued to touch upon during most of his journalistic career. With few exceptions, most of these texts also are listed or described in the outline he prepared for "The Way It Was," so we feel that we are following Colón's original intention to also collect and reprint some of these sketches in his unpublished book.

In transcribing and/or translating some of the material from the typescript drafts found among Colón's papers, we have made minor stylistic, grammatical and typographical corrections to the originals, trying very carefully not to betray in any way Colón's style or the essence of the original texts. Most of the essays have been annotated with explanatory information that the editors felt would enhance the understanding of a particular text. Three of the essays in Part II have been translated from their Spanish originals.

Needless to say, this project would not have been possible without the encouragement and support of the Recovering the U. S. Hispanic Literary Heritage Project coordinated by the University of Houston and Arte Público Press and funded in great part by the Rockefeller Foundation. The project's financial support greatly facilitated our research as well as our ability to meet and narrow the distance caused by being at two different academic institutions. Our gratitude to Nicolás Kanellos for his vision in creating the Recovering the U. S. Hispanic Literary Heritage Project and to Teresa Marrero, former Project Coordinator, for always lending a sympathetic ear and keeping things running efficiently and smoohtly.

We also would like to express our appreciation to the Centro Library staff for their invaluable assistance in locating and reproducing materials. Our special thanks to Nelly Cruz, Nélida Pérez and Amílcar Tirado. This project would not have been completed without their special assistance or without the enthusiasm and hard work of several graduate students from the Department of Latin American and Caribbean Studies (LACS) at the University at Albany, SUNY. Special recognition must be given to Andy Tishman, who became so enraptured by Colón's historical figure that he devoted his M.A. project to the study of Colón's life and works. A great deal of the bibliographical information in this volume is a result of Andy's perseverance and hard work. Our appreciation also goes to Betsy Campisi, Kimberly Miner and Sandra Pullyblank, who helped with some of the clerical aspects of the manuscript.

Finally, we are grateful to each other for sharing the same collective spirit of solidarity, love for our people and intellectual concerns that were so characteristic of Jesús Colón's life. Just like him, it is our hope that this effort contributes to motivating others in the future to begin where we leave off and to sustain the never-ending quest of recovering the legacies of our respective Latino communities.

Edna Acosta-Belén   *Virginia Sánchez Korrol*

The Way It Was
and Other Writings

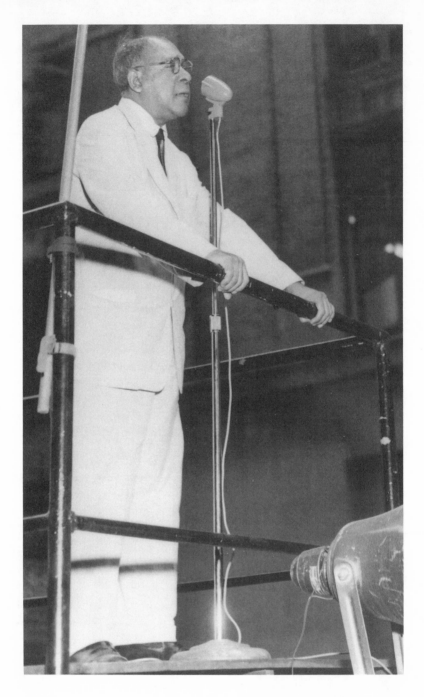

1: Jesús Colón, circa 1940s

The World of Jesús Colón

Historical Introduction

The Puerto Rican world of Jesús Colón encompassed the Island and the continental United States between 1901, the year of his birth, and 1974, the year of his death. It was populated by individuals who traveled between both geographic points in search of better economic conditions. A demographic breakdown of Puerto Rican migrants prior to World War II reveals that they were at their most productive years, that there were slightly more males than females, more from urban than from rural backgrounds, more whites than blacks and more likely skilled or semi-skilled in a trade. By mid-century, seasonal migrants hired to work in the agricultural fields of the eastern coastal states joined other Puerto Ricans displaced by the Island's industrialization program, Operation Bootstrap in sizeable migratory waves searching for expanding economic horizons.

In terms of skills and education, the post-war migrants compared favorably with those who remained behind. Exit ramp surveys conducted at the San Juan International Airport indicate a predominant representation of persons with experience in urban living, more years in school than the Island average and familiarity with non-agricultural employment. In other words, the men and women who shared Colón's world were the best *Borinquen* had to offer, and the absence of their productivity would subsequently have an impact on the Island's future.

While ultimately the decision to leave rested upon individual shoulders, it was conceived within a broader political and economic context that encouraged the displacement of what was considered excess population within a U. S. capitalistic orbit. Undoubtedly, all of the men and women who succumbed to the lure of continental shores sought to make a better life for themselves than what was promised in the homeland. Each contemplated a personal odyssey, believing he or she relocated for a constellation of private justifications. But the common ground in each of their experiences

13

was rooted in the Island government's inability to provide a future for an impoverished population.

If we acknowledge the population estimates by agencies such as the New York Mission Society for the migration of the 1920s and 1930s, the *colonia hispana* may well have numbered over 100,000 individuals. U. S. citizens since 1917, Puerto Ricans predominated among a diverse population of Spanish-speaking persons from Cuba, Venezuela, Mexico, Colombia, Spain and the Dominican Republic. As U. S. citizens, however, Puerto Ricans often failed to appear in immigration statistics and it was difficult to ascertain their exact numbers from other indicators. However, as census records became more inclusive, we learn that 53,000 individuals living in the United States in 1930 were Puerto Rican. During the period of the Great Migration, as the massive exodus that followed on the heels of World War II was known, the numbers of U. S. Puerto Rican residents escalated from 69,967 in 1940 to 301,375 in 1950. Twenty years later, in the decade of the 1970s, they increased to 1,429,396, more than tripling their numbers.[1]

Focusing on early migrant life in the United States, Colón's compatriot and hometown friend, cigarmaker Bernardo Vega (1885-1965), was one of a handful of Puerto Rican writers that also included the Afro-Caribbeanist Arturo Alfonso Schomburg. All three chronicled the pre-World War II migration experience through their respective working class and racial perspectives, stressing the continuum of cohesive, vital communities, civic and political leadership, and working class activism. If there was a universal collective expectation for all those who migrated, Vega expressed it well while bound for New York on board the ship *Coamo* in 1916. Economic considerations and the dream of returning to the Island formed the recurring theme for many who left.

> The days passed peacefully. Sunrise of the first day and the passengers were already acting as though they belonged to one family. It was not long before we came to know each other's life story. The topic of conversation, of course, was what lay ahead: life in New York City. First savings would be for sending for close relatives. Years later the time would come for returning home with pots of money. Everyone's mind was on that farm they'd be buying or the business they'd set up in town ... All of us were building our own little castles in the sky.[2]

[1]Kal Wagenheim, *A Survey of Puerto Ricans on the U. S. Mainland in the 1970s* (New York: Praeger, 1975).

[2]César Andreu Iglesias, ed., *Memoirs of Bernardo Vega* (New York: Monthly Review, 1984): 5–6.

The core of Colón's Brooklyn community on the culmination of World War I centered around Myrtle Avenue, Columbia Street and the neighborhood around the Navy Yard. This area would serve as the stage for many of his earliest recollections at a time when the heart of *El Barrio Hispano* in Manhattan's Spanish Harlem was barely in formation. By the period between the World Wars, Puerto Ricans would live and work in communities that straddled the East River with well-defined Hispanic neighborhoods or *colonias* in both the Brooklyn and Manhattan boroughs.

From the start, Puerto Rican neighborhoods were tightly-knit with internal leadership provided by local merchants, *bodegueros* (grocers), politicians, *boliteros* (numbers racket men), clergy and professionals. Through a complex and sophisticated associational structure, the *colonias* maintained cultural and sociopolitical cohesion, stressing language, religion and heritage, creating workers' beneficent societies and other vehicles for change and continuity. As Colón delves into the activities of clubs like *Vanguardia* (Vanguard), the Liga Puertorriqueña e Hispana (Puerto Rican and Hispanic League), the Ateneo Obrero (Workers' Athenium), the Alianza Obrera (Workers' Alliance), and countless labor lodges and movements, his essays reflect an organizational network becomes more striking because it is absent from conventional literature on U. S. Puerto Ricans. Such discourses tended instead to downplay and misinterpret the significance and maturity of Puerto Rican interaction and group formation.

Well before setting foot on Brooklyn piers, Puerto Rican workers were already familiar, not only with unions and labor organizing, but with Socialist Party politics. Since 1899, the Federación Libre de Trabajadores (Free Federation of Workers), with its prominent assemblage of erudite tobacco workers, set the standards for promoting a complex working class agenda. Practices like *la lectura*, the custom of reading aloud to the cigar workers as they engaged in the specialties of their trade, flourished in Puerto Rican, and later New York, cigar factories. It provided a forum for the dissemination of critical knowledge while raising workers' consciousness about their solidarity with other laborers throughout the world, the equality of women and a myriad of other political issues. Both Colón and Vega experienced it firsthand and later wrote about this custom. Hired by the workers themselves, the designated *lector* (reader) focused the morning's presentation on current news and world events, while the afternoon highlighted more substantial literary fare, creating thereby the most enlightened men and women among the working class.

In spite of the ephemeral undercurrents of the migrant dream of returning to Puerto Rico once some degree of financial security was achieved, many Puerto Ricans were here to stay. And many more joined the cyclical migration that connected the Island and the U. S. communities, not unlike a geographic revolving door. The importance of building solid communities, assiduously documented in Colón's writings, coupled with the need to nego-tiate and protect individual civil liberties and *lo puertorriqueño*, the Puerto Rican character permeated the community's formal and informal organiza-tional structure. By so doing, shared values and solidarity cut across class and racial lines.

Community organizations, including fraternal lodges and social clubs, brokered the politics of the *colonias* and, while many looked towards Puerto Rico for their inspirations, others confronted the socioeconomic status of the stateside community. Midway through the decade of the 1920s, at least forty-three Puerto Rican and Spanish-speaking civic, political or cultural organizations were already operating in the hearts of the Brooklyn and Man-hattan *colonias*. These confronted a wide-ranged agenda that included the day-to-day problems migrants faced in adjusting, celebrating and sustaining cultural heritage, supporting radical party politics on relevant continental issues and advocating for the self-determination and interests of Puerto Rico and other Latin American nations.

Puerto Ricans proved to be eclectic in their politics. Community-supported Democratic, Independent or Republican Party clubs kept abreast with the question of status for the Island with great interest and supported candidates who included Puerto Rico in their platforms. But, from its incep-tion *El Barrio* was also home to a significant contingent of left-wing organi-zations. "Harlem was a Socialist Bastion," declared Bernardo Vega, writing about the decade of the 1920s in his memoirs. Puerto Ricans, Spaniards and other Hispanics supported clubs like El Centro Obrero (The Workers' Center) which served as a source for Communist activity, the American La-bor Party and numerous radical workers' organizations. Colón himself was a candidate to the State Assembly and the Senate on the American Labor Party ticket. During the McCarthy era, Colón was investigated by the House Un-American Activities Committee.

Of all the politicians cited by Colón in his writings, none captured the imagination as forcibly as Vito Marcantonio. A champion of the working class and of independence for Puerto Rico, Marcantonio represented the radical politics with which Colón identified throughout the 1930s and 1940s. As a "friend of the poor, of the Puerto Ricans and of Puerto Rico, as well as the Spanish-speaking community," Marcantonio garnered the political support of the New York Puerto Ricans.[3] Given the dismal socioeconomic prospects and the discrimination that continued to plague the Puerto Rican

[3]*La voz* (September 20, 1939).

community, the politician had a great deal to fight for.

The reality of daily life for Puerto Rican migrants translated into a struggle to survive on meager wages, inadequate health care, sub-standard housing, marginal education and poor sanitation conditions. The growth and dispersal of the community by mid-century, coinciding with an increasing decline in manufacturing and related industries, gave rise to additional concerns. As the Operation Bootstrap industrialization program forced thousands to leave for the United States, primarily to New York and its immediate surroundings, Puerto Ricans remained locked in the lowest-paying and most unstable economic sectors. The steady trickle and advancements of second- and third-generation Puerto Ricans into white collar employment and the professions, most evident throughout the 1960s and 1970s, could not offset disproportionate representation in manufacturing and service occupations.

If climbing up the occupational ladder proved elusive, integration into U. S. institutions and its socioeconomic system was similarly fraught with color-coded barriers. Race and ethnicity factors permeated all levels of the migration experience. Although socioeconomic mobility was easier for white Puerto Ricans than for their racially mixed or black compatriots, identity was forged primarily along cultural rather than racial terms. Representing a society with a tradition of widespread interracial relationships, the color spectrum of Puerto Ricans ranged from white to black with many gradations in between, often found within the same family unit. As with other Latin American or Caribbean groups, racial identity for Puerto Ricans was categorized in ways more complex than the white/black paradigm observed in the United States.

Finally, the stability of the traditional barrios began to crumble when neighborhood revitalization programs appeared. Urban renewal precariously compromised the migrant's most basic needs and meant that older, previously stable Puerto Rican barrios faced substantial destruction and displacement. Residents relocated, but, with cheap housing virtually unattainable, resources available in internal communal support structures soon proved inadequate. To compound the problem, the public schools, traditional gateways for social mobility, were hard pressed to incorporate the soaring numbers of non-English speaking students who comprised a significant percentage of the migration.

As was the case in the years between the two world wars, the history of Puerto Ricans in the United States can be told through its organizational structure, for it is here in united social activism that the community lays claim to its human, civil and cultural rights. As Colón attacked the conditions affecting Puerto Ricans through his writings, other Puerto Rican leaders of the 1920s and 1930s joined forces in seeking new solutions to empower the community in its times of crisis. Together they were committed to developing leadership, unionizing workers and politicizing the barrios. A major difference between group formation or organizational structure after the 1950s was that earlier organizations tended to coalesce around the internal dynamics of a somewhat contained community, while the later groups responded to the dispersal of the people by projecting a city-wide (and later a national) focus.

By 1948, the New York office of the Migration Division of the Department of Labor of Puerto Rico strived to alleviate migrant adjustment problems, focusing especially on employment, housing and education. Monitoring the migrant flow from Puerto Rico, the agency attempted to lessen their impact on the city's infrastructure by diverting them to other regions of the country. Subsequently, the Migration Division became a significant but controversial mediator for the Puerto Rican community, sometimes encouraging and at other times inhibiting the formation of a city-wide agency with important political dimensions. An adjunct of the Island's commonwealth government, the Division's agenda was often viewed as compromised.

The emergence of local, state and national organizations, committed to improving urban living conditions, along with a strong Puerto Rican presence in workers' movements, underscored the community's resilience and maturation. Frequently aided by anti-poverty funding, the organizations of the 1950s and 1960s promoted community interests and also produced an identifiable cadre of leaders. From the small group of teachers entrenched in the public school system, who advocated for bilingual education and decentralization, to public servants, health care workers and social workers, the community was on the move.

In the mid-1950s, the Puerto Rican Forum marshalled the human resources of the community to assess its problems and to draft blueprints for their solutions. The Forum sought to provide a wide range of social services, to nurture a leadership body that could represent Puerto Ricans and other Latinos at local, state and regional levels and in private or public institutions. The founding of ASPIRA in 1961 turned the spotlight towards education, while the Puerto Rican Family Institute implemented an agenda in 1963 geared to the delivery of badly needed social services. The Puerto Rican Community Development Project in 1965, a comprehensive consortium of organizations, complemented a score of local groups that coalesced around specific concerns. These included neighborhood groups, housing and block associations, social and hometown clubs, cultural societies and senior citizens' councils.

In the wake of the civil rights movement, Puerto Ricans resumed a radical agenda reminiscent of the left-wing politics of an earlier era. The militancy of the 1960s mobilized Puerto Rican youth to challenge the establishment through confrontational intervention. They sought to right the wrongs inflicted on the community. Impatient with the sluggish gains achieved through more conventional methods, The Young Lords, the Puerto Rican Socialist Party (PSP), El Comité (The Committee) and the Puerto Rican Students' Union channelled the energies of the second generation, born and raised in the barrios, into action. They took to the streets to protest police brutality, discrimination, inhumane living conditions, poverty and neglect in education, health and sanitation. The more militant took over abandoned buildings where they established breakfast programs for school children, coerced medical facilities into providing basic health care for the ill, and other programs for survival. Puerto Rican youths demanded their rightful place at universities and helped to establish departments and programs of Puerto Rican Studies throughout the City (CUNY) and State (SUNY) University of New York systems. Puerto Ricans considered such administrative programs as open admissions at the university and access to instruction in one's own native language through bilingual education programs were rights of citizenship rather than concessions.

While the groups differed with regard to orientation and strategies, they agreed on several fundamental issues. These included the independence of Puerto Rico and underscored the continuation of inextricable bonds between the U. S. and the Island communities. They understood their position of "children of a forced migration" and as "victims of racism" and economic exploitation.

As Jesús Colón's Puerto Rican world came to an end, many of the ideals, values and struggles in which he engaged remained vibrant and alive. He did not live to see the demographic explosion caused by the tremendous increase in the Spanish-speaking immigrants during the 1970s and 1980s with its potential for transnationalizing the sociocultural and political fabric of the United States. Yet, through his written legacy Jesús Colón continues to empower the Puerto Rican community. His documentation of the neglected pages of our history lays the foundation for its survival.

The Man and His Writings

In 1917, at the age of sixteen and the year before he left Puerto Rico for New York as a stowaway, (see the Biographical Chronology), Jesús Colón began his long and passionate career as a writer when he assumed the editorship of the newspaper *Adelante* at the Central Grammar School in San Juan. It is fervently established in his first editorial that the neophyte journalist from the tobacco-growing countryside of Cayey was keenly aware that words and writing were potentially effective tools for transforming society. Most of all, and aside from what became a lifelong love affair with writing, Colón recognized that his words might have a transcending, enduring and inspirational effect on younger generations. As he remembered forty years later in one of his newspaper columns *As I See It From Here*, the Central Grammar School was also the site of his first strike, the place where he victoriously led his American History classmates into boycotting class until the North American teacher rescinded an order that would force each student to pay ten cents for the history textbook that had disappeared from the teacher's desk the day before.[4] These early experiences help us define Colón's fundamental profile: an individual of profound social consciousness and, foremost, a deep believer in communitarianism and in achieving social and political change through collective action. He continued to adhere to this philosophy when he migrated to New York City. Shortly after his arrival, he became a founding member of the first New York Committee of the Puerto Rican Socialist Party and was deeply involved in the social and political organizing of a growing Puerto Rican *colonia*.

Colón's passion for writing is substantiated by his prolific output during more than five decades of journalistic activity. Our research has led us to identify more than four hundred pieces of writing scattered over more than thirty different newspapers, magazines and newsletters of community, labor or political organizations, and the search is still far from complete (see the Bibliography). But Colón was not by any means a mainstream journalist. First of all, he was a self-educated man who did not complete formal secondary schooling until he was a working adult (see "Jesús is Graduating Tonight"). His working class origins and involvement during his formative years in an intensively militant socialist labor movement in Puerto Rico combined with his own personal struggles as a destitute migrant in New York City to turn him into an irrepressible voice of the working class. It could be said that he developed his journalistic craft directly from the trenches, from the University of Life, as he himself would say.[5] Since his early years in New York, he became a frequent writer for labor newspapers and other community organization publishing outlets. During more than fifty years, he was able to consistently represent the concerns of his times through the

---

[4]Colón recounts this incident in "My First Strike" included in *A Puerto Rican in New York and Other Sketches*, 2nd edition (New York: International Publishers, 1982): 15–16. The sketch was originally published in *The Daily Worker* (February 26, 1957).

[5]Colón was a believer that life itself was comparable to an eternal university. For him a life of struggle was a life of learning. This philosophy is a reflection of his revolutionary socialist ideology in which theory and praxis are inseparable. See "De la Universidad de la Vida: Apuntes iconoclastas para la página universitaria," *Summer School News* (University of Puerto Rico, August 13, 1928): 10.

weekly pages of *Justicia*, *Gráfico* (published 1927–1931), *Pueblos hispanos* (1943–1944), *Liberación* (1946–1949), *The Daily Worker* (1924–1958), *The Worker* (1958–1968), *The Daily World* (1968–1986) and *Mainstream*, to mention only a few of these publications.

In 1923, almost five years after his arrival in the United States, Colón began writing regularly when he became one of the New York correspondents to *Justicia*, the official newspaper of the Federación Libre de Trabajadores (FLT) in Puerto Rico.[6] During the 1920s and 1930s he was also a regular columist for several Spanish newspapers in New York City, among them Bernardo Vega's *Gráfico*. In the 1940s, he wrote primarily for *Pueblos hispanos*, a weekly founded by Puerto Rican nationalist poet Juan Antonio Corretjer, and for *Liberación*, a publication founded by anti-fascist Spanish exiles in New York. The bulk of his writing is constituted by his journalistic essays which, because of their intensily human interest and anecdotal style, often read more like short stories than mere pieces of social criticism or informative reporting. In his early years, Colón also published scattered poems in some of the same publications metioned above. For what appears to be primarily humoristic reasons, he ocassionally used the pennames of Tiquis Miquis and Pericles Espada.[7]

As noted in the first section of our essay, for the Puerto Rican community in New York, the 1940s and 1950s represented the period of largest population growth. The significant population increases during these years made Puerto Ricans in New York a more visible, but not necessarily a more welcome presence. Since his early years in New York, Colón had witnessed the racial and ethnic tensions that to this day still characterize U. S. urban life. As the community grew, discrimination often took the form of physical violence or vandalism against Puerto Ricans and the community's small businesses. Racial violence came from the white society as much as it did from other ethnic groups in the City. Within this hostile environment the need for support systems and a unified community became increasingly ap-

[6]A few months after the U. S. invasion of Puerto Rico, island workers saw the need to centralize the many small unions into a larger organization. The short-lived *Federación Regional de los Trabajadores de Puerto Rico* (FRT) emerged from these efforts and helped intensify labor activism on the Island. Less than a year later, because of the pressures exerted by the various political parties trying to control the organization, there was a split in the organization that led to the creation of the *Federación Libre de Trabajadores* (FLT). In 1901, the FLT became an affiliate of the American Federation of Labor, increasing the linkages between U. S. and Island labor activism.

[7]Colón used the pseudonym of Tiquis Miquis in the section "En Neoyorkino" which he wrote for the newspaper *Gráfico* during the period between May 5, 1927, and May 4, 1928. He used the pseudonym Pericles Espada while writing a series of letters under the rubric "Cartas Inmorales a Mi Novia" also published in *Gráfico* between August 5, 1928, and December 28, 1928.

parent, bringing about the creation of numerous grassroots organizations. Colón was one of the key figures in this process by becoming a founding member of the Alianza Obrera Puertorriqueña (founded in 1922), the Ateneo Obrero Hispano (1926) and the Liga Puertorriqueña e Hispana (1928). These organizations fostered mutual aid, collective struggle and solidarity among Puerto Ricans and other Latinos, and enriched the early community's social and cultural life. In his writings Colón records many of these events and shows a clear determination to honor the deep traditions and strivings of working-class Puerto Ricans in establishing their New York communities and in the pursuit of a better life for themselves and their families.

It was in the mid-1950s when Colón began writing columns in English for *The Daily Worker* (the name later changed to *The Worker* and *The Daily World*), a socialist workers' newspaper.[8] This association with the newspaper and later on with the American Labor and Communist Parties, the latter which he had joined almost two decades before, were also central to all of his life activities. As a result of his involvement with the socialist labor movement, Puerto Rican pro-independence groups and the Communist Party, both as a political activist and through his journalistic work, he was the subject of an investigation during the McCarthy Era by the House Un-American Activities Committee (HUAC). His statement before the Committee attests to Colón's strong convictions regarding the illegality of U. S. colonial domination of Puerto Rico and his commitment to independence for the Island.[9] However, as mentioned earlier, his introduction to socialist ideals had come much earlier, during his youth in Puerto Rico where, in 1915, he had joined the ranks of the FLT and of its political organ, the Puerto Rican Socialist Party founded in his beloved Cayey. Because of the large number of U. S. absentee landowners, combined with the presence of one of the largest military camps on the Island, the countryside town of Cayey exemplified U. S. colonial domination of Puerto Rico. Thus for Colón, these formative

[8]Radical labor journalism in the United States was flourishing during the time Colón migrated to New York from Puerto Rico, partly as a result of the triumph of the Bolshevik Revolution. On February 2, 1922, *The Worker* first appeared as a weekly publication and served as an advance agent to *The Daily Worker*, which began publication in January 13, 1924. The *Daily Worker* appeared for thirty-four years, making it the longest published labor newspaper in the United States. On January 19, 1958, it was suceeded by *The Worker*, which ceased publication in June 25, 1968, and by the *Daily World*, which first appeared on July 4, 1968. These publications followed the tradition established by many of the "Negro" weeklies of the post World War I era and the abolitionist press of the mid-nineteenth century. See "A New Paper with a 46 Year Tradition," *The Worker* (June 25, 1968): 9.

[9]In two of his *As I See It From Here* columns, Colón describes his experience after he was subpoened to testify for this congressional committee. See his articles "I Appear Before the UnAmericans," *The Worker* (December 29, 1959): 10; and "The UnAmericans and the Americans," *The Worker* (December 6, 1959): 10.

years and awakening experiences on the Island essentially molded his world view and had an enduring effect on his life as part of the New York emigré community. During his last two decades, Colón plunged into the world of electoral politics by becoming a political candidate first in 1953, when he ran for the New York City Council, and then a year later as a candidate for the New York State Assembly on the American Labor Party ticket. Another failed attempt as a political candidate came in 1969 when he ran for New York City Controller under the Communist Party ticket.

The fact that the bulk of Colón's writings ended up being in English, rather than in his native Spanish, illustrates his determination to continuously educate himself and improve his skills in his second language, which eventually became his basic survival tool. He, like many other Puerto Ricans before and after him, took any available job that would eventually allow him to bring his family from the Island. Therefore, the migrant experience turned Colón into a jack-of-all-trades, working at different points in time as a dishwasher, messenger, night porter, dock worker, factory worker, postal clerk, labor organizer, teacher and lecturer. However, writing was not only his passion, but an ongoing activity throughout his life. Being primarily a self-educated man, he often expressed both a moral and practical obligation to improve himself in the art and science of writing in the English language.[10]

In his Foreword to the 1982 edition of *A Puerto Rican in New York and Other Sketches*, Juan Flores underscores the importance of Colón's writings as foreshadowing the literature written in English by second generation Puerto Ricans in the United States which began to emerge during the late 1960s. Along with this younger generation of writers, Colón represents the voice of those Puerto Ricans who have made their lives in the U. S. metropolis. Flores also stresses the importance of Colón's work which, together with the *Memorias de Bernardo Vega*, are still part of only a handful of the glimpses that we have of the New York Puerto Rican community prior to the great migration of the 1950s.

The apparent simplicity of Colón's English prose occasionally can be misleading to the reader. His sketches tend to be brief, but intensely profound and moving. Behind the unaffected and colloquial language that characterizes his anecdotal style, there is a man of strong social convictions and great wisdom. He comes through as a persuasive, compassionate, humorous and, at times, even ironic voice representing the disenfranchised in their claims for justice, equality and social change. But most of all, he has the uncanny ability to blend everyday simplicity and common sense with

---

[10]When Colón was attending Boys High Evening School, he wrote two assignments for his English class about the art of writing. These are included among his papers.

profound human and intellectual concerns. Thus Colón's writings cannot be understood apart from the ardent socialist ideology he had embraced during his formative years in Puerto Rico. In many ways his sketches reveal the qualities of an unassuming and honest man committed to doing his best to make the world a better place. What Colón learned from the working class activism and solidarity of the *tabaqueros* (cigar makers) during his Cayey childhood and from that "voice through the window" of the *lector* (reader) in the cigar factory near his house was marked in his memory for the rest of his life, plunging him into a similar role when, through his own writings, he became the sustaining voice committed to raising the consciousness of his Puerto Rican community.[11]

Colón is a master of the anecdotal or testimonial essay, following in the tradition still much alive within contemporary Latin American letters, but virtually discarded in the United States since the era of Mark Twain. By writing personal essays on public subjects, he identifies his own experiences with those of the whole community. At times we hear his outbursts of anger or indignation at any kind of social injustice, but this outrage never turns into a paralyzing pessimism. Even in the face of the worst social ills and human rights violations that he so frequently addresses in his writings, Colón never waivers in his belief in the people's capacity to achieve revolutionary change. In describing Colón's anecdotal and didactic style, Sidney Finkelstein notes that he talks "not only to the working people alone, nor to the Puerto Rican people alone, but to the American people as a whole."[12]

Colón is a model of the self-made erudite who learned as much from books as he did from daily life experiences. Within his limited scope of educational opportunities, he was always seeking to expand his knowledge and understanding of the world. He completed high school as an adult, attending evening classes at Brooklyn's Boys High School (see "Jesús is Graduating Tonight") and later in his life, completed two years of college at St. Johns University.

As a committed socialist, he was a great believer in humanity and the possibility of revolutionary change through collective action. This is exemplified by his tireless involvement in a whole array of grassroots organizations and groups in which he became a pivotal and sustaining force during

[11]It was a common practice in the cigar-making shops or factories of the period to have a *lector* or reader to entertain the workers who was also paid by the workers themselves. Colón underscores the importance of the reader in his life in "A Voice Through the Window," included in *A Puerto Rican in New York and Other Sketches*, 11–13. The *lector*'s job was to read from daily newspapers, working class publications or from major classics of literature or political thought. According to Colón, this individual was a combination of orator and actor and was usually connected to the Island's socialist movement.

[12]Review, *A Puerto Rican in New York, Political Affairs* 41:1 (1962): 63–65.

the early years of New York City's Puerto Rican *colonias*. In 1944, Colón became a labor organizer for the Sociedad Fraternal Cervantes, the Spanish Section of the International Workers Order, a multinational organization of more than 180,000 members, where he was in charge of some thirty Spanish- and Portuguese-speaking lodges throughout the United States. These organizations promoted the involvement of children and young adults in artistic, cultural and sports activities.

Colón's working class origins, social consciousness and social beliefs provided the fundamental texture to his coherent socio-historic analysis of the migrant experience and of the colonial condition of Puerto Rico and its people. He had a keen understanding of the multiplicity of oppressions based on class, race, ethnic and gender differentiations inherent in the capitalist and colonial systems which prevailed within U. S. society. His advocacy of social justice and freedom for Puerto Ricans came to him with the same ease and fervor with which he would defend the civil rights struggles of African-Americans and women's rights, or express his indignation against McCarthyism, antisemitism, racism, Latin American and Spanish repressive governments and police brutality.

As a whole, Colón's writings offer an incisive critical view of U. S. society. He admires the democractic foundations upon which this nation was built, but recognizes the betrayal of those principles by a capitalist system of accumulation that perpetuates profound inequalities, exploits the workers and works against their well-being while keeping power and privilege in the hands of a wealthy few. In his sketch, "The Head of the Statue of Liberty," he perceives and poignantly captures the "credibility gap" between what the statue symbolizes and the struggles for freedom and justice that Puerto Ricans and other minority groups must confront in U. S. society. Colón's ties with the Puerto Rican socialist labor and independence movements kept his attention focused on the survival struggles of the laboring class and on his revolutionary dreams of social revindication and national liberation. An implacable enemy of injustice and inequality, he was also an advocate of working class empowerment and solidarity among the oppressed.

Being a Black Puerto Rican, Colón experienced racial prejudice, both on the Island and in the metropolis (see "Angels in My Hometown Church"), and was well aware that racism and segregation had a tormented and violent history and were deeply ingrained in the fabric of U. S. and Puerto Rican so- ciety. Several of his writings capture some of the darkest pages of U. S. racial history as well as of the fledging civil rights movement. In these sketches he continuously stresses the importance for Puerto Ricans of recognizing their own African heritage. Colón was also a great admirer of his *compatriota* Arturo Schomburg, whom he had known and worked with since the 1920s through many shared community organizations and activities.[13] He recognized and praised Schomburg's extraordinary dedication to developing an archival collection of the Black experience worldwide and underscored the importance of his work not only for the African-American community, but also for the Puerto Rican community (see "Arthur Schomburg and Negro History"). It is not then surprising that Colón emulated Schomburg's lifelong work as a bibliophile by also collecting and leaving behind a rich legacy of newsletters, leaflets, periodical articles, news clippings, journals, books, reports, photographs and correspondence that have become so valuable in the reconstruction of the history of the Puerto Rican community. These materials are now part of the Jesús Colón Papers Collection at the Centro de Estudios Puertorriqueños Library at Hunter College.

Although Colón remained in New York for more than five decades (1917–1974) and returned only occasionally to his native Island, Puerto Rico and his people always remained with him in everything he did and wrote. Many of his sketches are remembrances of incidents and characters from his hometown of Cayey. In his sketch, "The *Fanguito* Is Still There," he shares his outrage with his second wife Clara as they look at the urban destitution of slum dwellers in the Island's capital of San Juan.[14] Some of the human interest characters and stories found in those writings dealing with the Island also surface when he is back in the neighborhood streets of New York, capturing the many ways in which ordinary people lived their daily lives. But Colón was also an internationalist, a fact that allowed him to recognize the interconnectedness between the Island and U. S. communities and the shared struggles of working people all over the world who confronted colonial displacement and marginalization. His newspaper columns were not limited to local community affairs. He continuously kept his readers abreast of what was happening in Latin America, Spain and other parts of the world, making the necessary connections among the struggles for human advancement and liberation worldwide.

There is a striking ideological consistency to what Colón writes, to the

[13]Schomburg came to New York in 1891 at the age of seventeen and died in 1938. In his *Memorias de Bernardo Vega*, given in note 2, Vega also pays tribute to Schomburg's contributions: "He came here as an emigrant and bequeathed a wealth of accomplishments to our countrymen and to North American Blacks. What a magnificent example of solidarity among all oppressed people!" (196). For more information on Schomburg's life, see Victoria Ortiz, "Arthur Schomburg: A Biographic Essay/Arturo Schomburg: Un ensayo biográfico," *The Legacy of Arthur Alfonso Schomburg: A Celebration of the Past, A Vision for the Future* (New York: Schomburg Center for Research on Black Culture, 1986): 18–117.

[14]Colón married twice. In 1925 he married a Puerto Rican woman from his hometown, Rufa (Concha) Concepción Hernández, who joined him in New York. After her death, he married Clara Colón, a Jewish-American writer, educator and activist in the National Women's Coalition of the Communist Party.

subjects and themes that attract him. For him, writing was a didactic and consciousness-raising tool about class, racial and gender oppression as much as the means to forge a historical record and tradition for his community. It is in this regard that Colón should be considered a historical visionary of sorts, an *adelantado* (trailblazer) of his time—one of those exceptional figures who recognized the tremendous importance of defining a Puerto Rican tradition in New York that would remain as a source of inspiration and resistance for the many generations of migrants that might come after him. In many ways, he anticipated the social revindication and cultural revitalization struggles that, since the late 1960s, have come to characterize the various ethnic and women's movements in the United States and all over the world. A man of profound social consciousness, strong convictions and clear sense of purpose, Colón understood that the history of the Puerto Rican working class which was developing in the U. S. metropolis through the migration process would not be recorded by the cultural elite. It was up to working-class people like himself to provide his fellow *compatriotas* with that voice, to speak with the authority of experience in the everyday struggles for survival in the face of poverty and discrimination in the metropolis while building their own communities.

Colón always intended his writing to help counteract the prevailing misconceptions and biased views of the Puerto Rican people held by the larger U. S. society. He was tireless in his effort to teach the community about their progressive leaders and writers, to point out the affinities among Puerto Ricans and other oppressed groups and to celebrate the spirit of solidarity and enduring experiences of the early pioneers.

In *A Puerto Rican in New York and Other Sketches*, Colón had recognized the need to provide the U. S. public with a different view of how Puerto Ricans really lived and what their cultural contributions were to "the cultural advancement of the Western hemisphere, including that of the United States" (1982, 10). His unfinished *The Way It Was* was conceived along similar lines. From the working book outlines found among his papers, it can be concluded that the structure and format of the manuscript were not to differ significantly from *A Puerto Rican in New York*. The major difference was that *The Way It Was* was meant to be a more extensive and encompassing historical project. In examining the outlines, it becomes immediately apparent that *The Way It Was* was also to be a testimonial account of the evolution of the Puerto Rican community in New York and of its major figures and organizations. It was Colón's way of paying tribute to the strength, spirit of survival and solidarity and to the life experiences that he himself shared and endured with many other working class migrants in New York City. A large number of the essay items or ideas listed or described in the various versions of the book outline were not found among his papers and may never have been written. Many others, however, were to be reprinted from his published articles and columns, some of which already had appeared in *A Puerto Rican in New York*.

When Colón published *A Puerto Rican in New York*, he was very much aware that very little had been written about Puerto Ricans, besides the "voluminous studies and official reports" (1982, 9) that reduced them to statistical charts or to a major social problem. He was particularly taken aback by the negative or biased reporting of the U. S. mass media and the cheap sensationalism about the community that deprived Puerto Ricans of their humanity and undervalued their historical or cultural heritage and their presence in the United States. He was often critical of the ignorance that the U. S. public shared about one of its own colonial territories: "There is no inkling of our international outlook, our solidarities with the struggles of other peoples, especially our sense of identity with the peoples of Latin America. There is no hint of the deep traditions of striving for freedom and progress that prevade our daily life." Recognizing this reality, Colón was determined to demonstrate the truth about how most Puerto Ricans "feel, think, work and live" (1982, 10). Thus he is lending a voice to the "people without history," those who had been relegated to the margins of society and to whom history had been previously denied. At the same time, he is staking a claim for a space in which Puerto Ricans emerge as active participants and contributors to the development of their own U. S. communities and to the society at large.

In "The Library Looks at Puerto Ricans" (138–40), one of the sketches in *A Puerto Rican in New York*, Colón makes reference to a list of books about the Puerto Rican community disseminated by the New York Public Library and regrets that although ninety-five percent of the city's population is working class, this particular bibliography has no entries on trade unions or on Puerto Rican labor. He points to the wealth of materials he knew existed scattered through many newspapers and other kinds of community publications and fully recognizes that the historical invisibility of the working class had to be overcome to counterbalance the biased or distorted views of Puerto Ricans and give the younger generations a clear sense of self-worth and pride about their heritage.

Another of his *A Puerto Rican in New York* sketches, "Name in Latin," best summarizes Colón's awareness and commitment to the enterprise of recovering and preserving the historical record of the community. He tells the story of a Latin American printer and poet who wanted to start a weekly newspaper during the 1920s to combat the abuses and discrimination against the Latino community. He invited a group of friends, Colón among them, to decide on a name for the proposed publication. After much discussion, the group could not agree on a name and the prospective publisher suggested *Vae Victis* (*El ay de los vencidos* in Spanish; the cry of the vanquished in English). He finally convinced his friends of the desirability of this name, but when the first issue of *Vae Victis* was printed, hardly anyone bought it. The first issue was the last. As Colón tells us, "The Greeks thought it was a publication for the Italians, the Italians thought it was a magazine for the Romanians, the Romanians thought it was a paper for the French" (54). With his characteristic sense of humor and vision, Colón remembers what in retrospect seemed a foolish idea and laments that he did not keep a copy of the only issue, "a rare collector's item for the unknown researcher who will be writing the history of the Puerto Ricans in New York fifty years from now" (55).

It has been fifty years since Colón first recorded this anecdote. Nonetheless, we are now engaged in a search that Colón was able to foresee: bringing to light the chapters hidden in the history of the Puerto Rican migrant community, allowing for a richer and more enhanced self-identity and further enabling the process of reclaiming and defining its own cultural and historical space within U. S. society.

Colón once described the essence of his career in terms of four major activities, "leer, estudiar, organizar y luchar" (reading, studying, organizing and engaging in the struggle).[15] Nothing can better attest to this statement than his own writings, activism and leadership in more than twenty-five community organizations. They constitute his legacy, a very special way of *hacer patria* (constructing the nation) by passing along to the future generations of Puerto Ricans the inspiration he garnered from the words of the Antillean patriot José Martí, "El que tenga patria que la honre, y el que no, que la conquiste" ("Honor your country if you have one; and if you do not have one, struggle for it").[16]

Writing about Puerto Ricans who have come to New York to forge their lives in the metropolis, Colón's works and assuredly those of other yet undiscovered Puerto Rican men and women of the early community provide a sense of historical continuity and cultural legacy for the generations

---

[15]Colón was frequently honored for his contributions to the community by many of the organizations he helped to establish. On one of those ocassions, Mina Ortiz prepared some introductory remarks based on information provided to her by Colón. She begins her introductory remarks by characterizing Colón's life through these activities. A copy of her statement dated March 9, 1951, is found among the Jesús Colón Papers at the Centro Library.

[16]As quoted in the newspaper article "Fallece Jesús Colón, luchador por la libertad puertorriqueña," *Mundo Diario* (May 18, 1974).

to come.

Edna Acosta-Belén　　　　　　　　　　　*Virginia Sánchez Korrol*

Part I: *The Way It Was*

2: Puerto Rican community demonstration, 1940s

Castor Oil: Simple or Compound?

This happened to me the first week I was in New York (Brooklyn), over fifty years ago.

My working, useful, everyday English was almost non-existent. A first-year high school course, full of long declinations of the verb *to be* and tedious explanations of the difference between *shall* and *will*—differences that I still don't understand—was all the linguistic baggage I had to deal with Brooklynese.

That was the reason I felt almost tongue-tied the evening I went for a castor oil purgative at the old drugstore at Atlantic Avenue and Clinton Street. That drugstore, I later learned, had been at the same corner for the last hundred years.

I came to that store in desperation. Perhaps it was the food fed to me on the ship on which I came as a stowaway from San Juan, Puerto Rico. Perhaps it was the change of climate, maybe it was the cheap breakfast I'd had—a lump of cadaverous-colored, cold oatmeal, as hard as a baseball, served in a yellowish, cracked bowl whose crevices were pasted with dirt. This, followed by a watery cup of cold coffee, might have been the cause of that historic stomach ache during my first week in the United States. My belly was not the calm, serene, pleasant and obedient organ that I had known for years. The miracle of transforming a plate of rice and beans with an occasional morsel of meat into blood nerves and muscles had been religiously performed daily by my paunch without complaint, until that night. However, thin and flaccid, the end product always came out agreeably, but not that night.

Shortly after the evening meal, as tasteless a meal as the morning break-fast, comprising items my poor stomach was not accustomed to—*things* began to happen.

An internal rebellion threatened to become external any minute. A revolution to erupt from all available outlets of my body.

I was rooming at 101 Atlantic Avenue where for $1.50 a week I was provided with a dirty, greyish couch assumed with two beer-smelling blankets. The odor had been provided by previous roomers. The drugstore was a couple of blocks away. I ran and was able to reach the man just as he was about to close for the evening. As I ran swiftly into the drugstore holding my belly with both hands as if I were three months pregnant, the druggist asked me rhetorically: "What's ailing you?"

I detected a knowing smile on his face. "Castor oil," my answer was concrete and precise.

That was the purgative given to us by our grandmothers when I was a kid at Cayey, my home town in Puerto Rico. I also remembered its diabolic taste. But I didn't know any other purgative.

"Simple or compound?" the druggist asked in a simple business-like way.

"Compound?" Flashes of castor oil *compuesto* with ashes and other ingredients equally infernal, that I heard being administered to other boys in my childhood days, translated automatically the "compound" word.

"Simple," I say at last. The pharmacist was very obliging. He brought a nice, clean, tall glass and filled three quarters of it with pure, heavy, sluggish castor oil.

"Drink it." The pharmacist said. His words sounded half command and half plea.

The castor oil took its time to ramble from my mouth to the stomach in its slow, oily way. The oil seemed to be hanging for life to the walls of the esophagus from the tip of my throat to the distant bottom of my bowels. It was received down there more as an enemy than a friend.

It was a horrible drink, tough to get down. I drew a note of consolation when I congratulated myself for having chosen the castor oil simple, instead of the castor oil compound. Only my dead grandmother and the devil himself would have known all the fiendish oils and ashes that this yankee chemist would have mixed into the simple innocently crystal clear castor oil!

Compound, eh? Compound his yankee soul in the entrails of hell!

I had been clever enough to prevent the blondie apothecary from mixing my unadulterated castor oil with all the disgusting liquids and powders he must certainly have in hidden bottles and octagonal little boxes underneath his counter.

I paid and raced past the druggist to the top floor hall bathroom of the rooming house.

As I was flying uphill through the narrow stairs to my top floor cubicle, misnamed bedroom, I met the fat North American lady. She managed to squeeze herself down, while I was forcing myself up. For a moment, curiosity conquered the revolution in my bowels. In my halting English I explained to the landlady:

"I went to the drugstore. I ask 'castor oil.' He said 'simple or compound?' I said 'simple.' Can you tell me what would be if I said compound?"

The matronly-looking landlady could not stop a roar of laughter that shook the rickety old stairs. No doubt she was accustomed to buying castor oil for her children. After her loud laugh subsided, she patiently explained that castor oil compound is produced when the druggist uses less castor oil, mixes it with mint, vanilla, sasparilla, strawberry, and other tasty flavors that will make castor oil pleasant for the drinker to absorb.

She added gratuitously, "It is nicer than just plain castor oil."

I did not wait for further explanation. A good thing that the door to the communal toilet was wide open at the end of the hall. One minute more and . . . I made it just in time.

I don't remember just how long I sat there, notwithstanding the stream of thin snow filtering through the broken glass in the skylight above me and dropping on my hatless head.

I tiptoed to my room and sank in the beer-smelling couch. For hours I lay there half asleep, looking at the ceiling and waiting for nature to order me back to the cold toilet in the hallway.

Sometimes I was not lucky: when the one and only men's room was occupied by another roomer, I had to beat a careful retreat to my room and walk like a person dancing a slow tango. Incredible feats of will power helped me to wait until the most popular room in the hallway was free of human habitation.

What a night that was! I still remember it after so many years. During the long periods of semi-wakefulness on that couch, I dreamt of the English language classes conducted by the North American teacher. I remembered clearly the long periods of monotonous conjugations of *to be* which the teacher explained was the most important verb in the English language.

Standing in the very center in the front of the class he said: "Now, all together." And forty teenage voices repeated in unison, slowly and distinctly: "I am, You are, He is . . . " A pause. "We are, You are, They are . . . " This was repeated endlessly and collectively, in a kind of singsong which after a while produced a sort of somnolence.

All this time the teacher stood in front of us like the conductor of a third-rate symphony orchestra. The teacher's right hand was used in grandfather clock rhythmical movement that forced our heads to go along with the hand motion.

The long monotonous conjugation of a verb of a language most of us didn't want to learn, was followed by an " . . . explanation of the differences between the uses of shall and will." A difference that I have not understood to this date. That completed the teacher's daily effort to make us hate forever the language of Shakespeare and Whitman.

That night, when for the ninth time I had raced to the toilet, I sat and sat. The stomach seemed to have nothing else to get rid of. Still, I sat and waited, chin in hand, assuming the position of Rodin's famous statue. Talking to myself, I said aloud: "If instead of spending so much time on the verb *to be*, the teacher should have spent a few more minutes on the meaning of words like simple and compound ... "

And to tell you the truth, after so many years of struggling with the English language, I still don't know the difference between *shall* and *will*.

Jesús Is Graduating Tonight

The only one named Jesús at the June 1922 graduating class of the Boys High Evening School in Brooklyn was me.

That commencement evening was to be my last in the old brown building at Putnam and Marcy Avenues. After many long years of washing dishes, working on the docks, or at the many odd jobs in innumerable factories and shops where my hurried lunch hour was divided between a sandwich from home and the memorizing of geometric equations, I was going to graduate. The long days and evenings of work and study for a high school diploma had come to an end.

That graduation night will remain clearly in my mind until the day I die. I can still see some of my teachers sitting in the first row of the assembly hall where the ceremonies were to take place. The French teacher, with his *goatee* and *pince-nez*, looking like Georges Clemenceau. He used to tell me time and again not to give Spanish for French in his classes. The fourth-year English teacher, who on the basis of my essay, "The Automan as a Democratic Force in New York City," handed me the winner's prize: a copy of Shaw's *Man and Superman*.

The geometry teacher was tall, brisk, and serious, like a textbook on mathematics. I still remember his favorite saying: "I demand the homework be done. And if anybody doesn't like it, the door is open." And as he said this, his long arm to which was attached a long hand, from which pierced out a long ... (Whatever happened to all that geometry with which I struggled so valiantly and for which I spent so many sleepless nights?)

That graduating night all those teachers—and many others just as colorful—were sitting in the first row in the assembly hall. The rest of the auditorium was filled with relatives of the graduates, dressed that evening in their Sunday best.

The hard rolls of heavy white paper, imitation diplomas were handed to us. They were tied with bits of blue ribbon and were placed in an A-B-C order on the rectangular table on the stage. Our names were to be lettered-in later by an expert.

The graduating class was in a back room. I was wearing my older brother's blue serge suit. Each one of us practiced with Mr. Stone, the school principal, how our right hand would shake his right hand, while politely and gracefully we were to take our "diploma" with the left hand. My chest was expanding more than the usual; somebody in authority told me that I was the first Puerto Rican graduating from Boys Evening High. Boys High in those days was famous citywide in science and athletics.

Mr. Stone called me aside. "How do you pronounce your name in Spanish? I think it would be better to pronounce it in that language when I call you up," he said.

"Accent on the U, haysoos; not geesus, but haysoos." I responded.

Mr. Stone repeated after me several times: "haysoos, haysoos, haysoos" accenting it with a sharp nod of his head. After he did this exercise with my name over and over again, a radiant aura of triumph emerged on his pedagogical face as if he had just finished reading Don Quixote in its original language.

As our school band played the *Aida* "Triumphal March," we filed into our assigned seats on the stage. Patiently we heard the prominent politician's speech (What was his name?), who augured great things for all of us graduates. This was followed by the solo singer and the valedictory speech.

The time for awarding the "diplomas" had arrived. The principal went through the A's and the B's and part of the C's ... He wiped his forehead with a neatly folded handkerchief which, until that moment, had remained interred in the upper left pocket of his jacket. The principal cleared his throat. I knew I was next. "Geesus Colun." The principal's voice was loud and clear. He roared the English pronunciation of the best-known name in Christendom as if it had been shouted from a cathedral pulpit.

As the principal was shaking my hand, I noticed an almost imperceptible despair in his face as if to say "After all that practice ... "

As I was returning to my seat with my "diploma," someone in the audience said, sotto voce, "Even Jesus is graduating from high school tonight."

The Silent Contest

For years Carmen and Rosa had been exchanging gifts on their birthdays. The first year they exchanged just two things. But Carmen thought that Rosa was trying to show off by giving her something just a little fancier than the gift she gave Rosa. It just happened that Rosa felt that Carmen was trying to show off by giving a present a wee bit more expensive than the one she gave Carmen. Understand?

As the years passed and mutual birthdays piled upon mutual birthdays, this at first friendly competition, developed into a rapid contest. Larger and more expensive gifts were being presented between Carmen and Rosa. The rivalry grew to such an extent that the yearly birthday gifts soon required delivery by special messengers from the respective department stores. The old Puerto Rican precept—a very poor precept by the way—*no me voy a quedar da' (dado)*, was working in the conscience of both Carmen and Rosa. A loose translation of *no me voy a quedar da'* would be: "I am not going to let him or her put that over on me," or "If he or she punches me, I am going to punch him or her a bigger one." Or in simple terms, "He or she is not better than I am."

Carmen and Rosa continued to be friendly all through the years; but when their respective birthdays came, their smiles grew wider but forced.

After a few years of this friendly enemy-like birthday hypocrisy, the whole Puerto Rican neighborhood took notice of the fact. Everybody knew Carmen's and Rosa's birthdays, and an air of expectancy was in everybody's face as the truck from Ads, Macy's or Gimbel's stopped at Carmen's or Rosa's house on those days. The very curious went so far as to ask the truck driver's assistant, "What was in it?," as he was delivering the package.

In Carmen's or Rosa's living room you could find big fiery porcelain elephants with long, protruding ivory tusks, with savage looking tigers on their backs, or large cuckoo clocks with birds that had not cuckooed for many years, or a tall, thin porcelain jockey with no infusion of life—all scattered around for you to stumble over when you came in at night and the light was dim.

39

One good day, an old neighbor appeared in both their apartments. It was a day far in advance of both ladies' birthdays. He spoke to each of them separately, but in the same tone of voice and with the same content in his few words.

"You two grown-ups are acting like children. Every year when your birthdays come, you try to outdo each other in pomp and ostentation. Besides, you two are becoming the laughingstock of the neighborhood. Don't you think it is about time to stop this nonsense?"

Strangely enough, they listened attentively. Instead of telling the man, "Mind your own business," they both answered by saying, "But what shall I do?"

The man's advice to each of them was, "When the next birthday of your friend comes, just buy and send her a birthday card—the cheaper the better."

Then both of them started looking for the cheapest birthday card for the other's birthday, " ... the cheaper the better ... ," the man had said.

And the contest had begun again, but in reverse; hunting for the cheapest-looking birthday cards every year.

The Head of the Statue of Liberty[1]

I don't know why but, while looking at the head of the statue of liberty, I only discover in it a granite lifelessness. Scrutinize those eyes. They have a far off gaze as if the whole head is aiming at solving problems it hardly understands—problems of people far away beyond the seas and the oceans.

If that head could only turn around, just for a minute, and throw its freedom lights on the Harlem slums! If that head could only turn just a few blocks beyond the river and take a look at the Bowery!

Most of the people you see today laboriously climbing to the top of the Statue of Liberty are tourists. For them it is a "must!" Going to the top of the statue of liberty has become like another goal for a strong and athletic mountain climber anxious to stick his country's flag at the very peak for all the world to see.

We have a suggestion. That as the climbers are striving to reach the head of the statue, the voice of Paul Robeson[2] will be repeating in a tone of high fidelity:

> Give me your tired, your poor, your huddled masses yearning to breathe free, the wretched refuse of your teaming shore. Send these, the homeless, tempest-tossed, to me: I lift my lamp beside the golden door.

If Paul's voice unearths these great verses by Emma Lazarus now on a tablet inside the statue, its ringing words would sound as if they were really coming from the lips of the statue. And then the whole statue would be transformed from an empty lifeless symbol that seems to have joined the credibility gap into something living and meaningful for the black, Puerto Rican, Mexican American, Indian and poor white masses yearning and struggling for peace and freedom in this country today.

[1]Published in *The Daily World*, Magazine Section (July 27-28, 1968).
[2]African American singer born in 1898.

Nice to Have Friends in All Walks of Life

I think it was in the summer of 1943. One club, Vanguardia Puertorriqueña (Puerto Rican Vanguard), for years occupying a whole upper floor at
42 Smith Street, Brooklyn, was getting tired of small parks and small boats
for its annual picnic. That year we were almost forced to accept a fifteen-
hundred-passenger riverboat—The Pennsylvania—for our picnic at Bear
Mountain. After all, the *Vanguardia* was the best known and best organized
Puerto Rican club in Brooklyn during the early forties. Our reputation as a
still-growing organization was at stake.

Didn't we take P.S. 5 at Lawrence and Bridge Streets every year on
Mother's Day and fill its auditorium with more than a thousand mothers,
young and old, with their children and family? Didn't Marcantonio fly in
from Washington? Weren't Rev. Adam Clayton Powell, of Harlem fame,
and the Rev. Domingo Marrero, of the Puerto Rican Theological Seminary,
and many others, main speakers at our Mother's Day celebrations?[1] Didn't
we give a banquet to our Rafael Hernández,[2] composer of thousands of
popular songs, when he came to New York from his long stay in Mexico
City? Didn't the Vanguardia softball team win a championship at the national
softball competition in Chicago?

So these little picnic grounds and small boats for two or three hundred
persons were now out of the question. Thus we signed a contract for the
fifteen-hundred-passenger boat for ourselves alone—our members, their relatives and friends—which meant practically everybody.

If you are an old hand at picnic organizing, you know that the first thing
to do before deciding on a date is to find out what kind of weather you are
going to have. There are special weather maps which provide estimates of
the kind of weather expected months ahead.

I bought a copy of the map and woe—the only Sunday for which we could
contract The Pennsylvania was right in the middle of a two-month heavy

---

[1]See photograph no. 4.
[2]Black Puerto Rican composer (1892–1965) who lived in New York intermittently between
the 1920s and the 1940s.

rain. But the Vanguardia had to take it. Other nationalities, organizations and churches had taken all the other Sundays for their picnic outings. A predicted rainy Sunday was the only one left. And heaven forbid a year should pass without a picnic by the Vanguardia! ¡*Qué dirá la gente*! (What will people say!) ... That we were dying out! So we booked The Pennsylvania for the rainy Sunday.

As the executive representative of the club membership, I had to place one thousand twenty dollars in the captain's hand before he would give the order to sail from the Battery up the Hudson River to Bear Mountain.

That early Sunday morning was just as the three-month-ahead weatherman had indicated—foggy, windy, but still not raining.

We were to leave at nine in the morning, though the tickets read eight o'clock sharp. Most people going to picnics are ironically late.

I stood in front of the ship, dressed in a creamed-colored ensemble of pants and belted jacket, an exterior picture of affluence and confidence.

As the Puerto Ricans and other picnickers left the subway at Bowling Green and started to walk towards The Pennsylvania, I was counting every one of them. The human rush was not as heavy as I desired. My hope was that it wouldn't start really pouring before we had the ship on the way to Bear Mountain.

As the beer, soda, and ice are always paid for after the boat returns from the picnic, you can enjoy the luxury of ordering more than you estimate will be consumed on the trip.

Where our inexperience in renting large picnic ships was evidenced was in the ordering of the factory-prepared sandwiches and frankfurters. We ordered an exaggerated amount, especially of frankfurters. We forgot that it is customary for Puerto Rican families to bring most of their own food to picnics. They might buy an added delicacy like *bacalaos fritos* (small pieces of cod fish coated in white flour and fried in deep lard) or well-made *pasteles*, because it takes so much time and a lot of expertise to make a *pastel* (ground green plantains, condimented with meat, olives, capers, garlic, and other spices). We brought so many franks that we used them as balls to play baseball with on the deck of the ship on the return trip.

It was almost ten o'clock and I had around seven hundred dollars in my pocket from the sale of tickets. No more Puerto Ricans or other Hispanic picnickers were coming out of the Bowling Green-South Ferry subway station.

It meant that I had to procure an additional three hundred dollars within the next half hour if we were to leave for Bear Mountain at the latest moment, 10:30 A.M.

At the very moment that I was figuring out what to do, a Puerto Rican businessman and his family came driving up in his car to come to the picnic. He lived on the other side of the Brooklyn Bridge, about a fifteen minute drive. We were very good friends.

"You don't happen to have any money at home?" I asked before he had time to board the boat with his family.

"We happen to be a few hundred dollars short at the moment. We have to give the captain a thousand twenty dollars before we are allowed to start up the river." I added.

"How much money do you need?"

"About three hundred dollars."

The businessman left his family on the boat and drove back home; he returned in twenty minutes with three hundred dollars.

In the interim, a few more passengers came aboard The Pennsylvania and I was able to hand one thousand twenty dollars to the captain.

We were on our way.

The day was full of sun. Young and old mingled in joy and dancing. Puerto Rican *danzas* and waltzes were sandwiched between the foxtrots and rumbas raging at that time. The boat ballroom was spacious and waxy. There was singing and guitar playing all over the boat.

We caught a man who had brought dozens of pints of hooch in a burlap bag to sell all over the ship. We took them away from him and locked them up until the boat anchored at the Battery again.

We had reserved an area at Bear Mountain. We had baseball, sack and potato races, and a tug-of-war. We all became young again for a day.

There were minute instructions printed on the back of each ticket as to the time to be back on board the boat for our return trip. Reminders were broadcast over the Bear Mountain public address system, repeating the time everybody was supposed to be on the boat.

All but one complied. While everyone on board was shouting good-bye to imaginary friends along the deserted river shore, this man started to walk very slowly to the boat. As he was about to step onto the wooden plank connecting the land with the boat, he turned back, hopping and skipping, mimicking and clowning for the passengers from the shore. Then, he slowly walked back to the foot of the wooden plank and, pointing with his index finger, he moved it hesitantly as if saying, "No, No, No."

For the first few minutes the passengers laughed at the one man show on the shore. Every time the man stepped backward from the plank with an air of grave importance, there were guffaws and snickers, exploding into roars of laughter. But as time passed, there were shouts of ¡*Déjenlo ahí*! (Leave him there!).

Mothers with small children who wanted to get home before it was too dark became the more vociferous: Leave him there! Leave him there! *¡Qué payaso!* (What a clown!).

When the man saw the captain give the final order to draw the wooden plank into the ship, the man sprinted toward the boat. He was barely able to reach the wooden plank with the tip of his feet. For a moment we thought he was going to fall into the water, but he managed to achieve a balance. Then he ran onto the boat and rapidly mingled with the other passengers.

On the way down the river to the Battery, the Puerto Ricans continued eating crispy *bacalaítos.* The salt in the cod fish plus the almost continuous dancing to the tunes of the very good live music made them buy beer and more beer. In the middle of the trip home I called aside my businessman friend and paid back his three hundred dollars.

When we had reached about the 125th Street point in the river, rain started to pour.

Thunder, lightning and rain. It seemed that nature, though a little late in the day, wanted to certify that those who made the three-month-ahead weather map were not fly-by-night individuals.

The picnickers came from the open deck into the dry roomy parts of the boat. The middle-aged kept on asking the band for romantic Puerto Rican waltzes from the days when they were young. The youth formed ring-around-the-rosies, inside others continued to dance on the deck under the rain, singing the old Puerto Rican children's tune:

> *Que llueva, que llueva, la virgen de la cueva*
> *Los pajaritos cantan, la virgen se levanta ...*

over and over again.

There were kisses and hugs as we disembarked at the Battery. There were no good-byes. The words spoken were: *"Hasta el año que viene"* ("Until next year").

A Bright Child Asks a Question

Christopher Columbus discovered Puerto Rico on November 19, 1493, on his second voyage. The first two black slaves were brought to Puerto Rico from Spain in 1510. The Indians in Puerto Rico almost disappeared by the middle of the next century. The remaining Indians, the blacks and the whites who came in great numbers have been mixing and marrying each other in Puerto Rico for over four hundred years.

Although there undoubtedly remain some pure white and pure black families and some Indian-type persons, the races have merged to such an extent that it is difficult in many instances to detect the race to which a particular Puerto Rican belongs.

Which brings us to the story about a Puerto Rican progressive mother living in El Barrio, New York's largest concentration of Spanish speaking people—mostly Puerto Ricans.

The mother was teaching her child some of the songs heard among the Afro-Americans during those days. That day the mother was teaching her child "We Shall Overcome."

When the mother came to the words "black and white together," the little Puerto Rican girl asked, "Mother, what am I, black or white?"

He Couldn't Guess My Name

Coney Island is not what it used to be. The old Coney of Luna Park and Steeplechase are gone forever. So is the "parachute jump" where you were thrown head first from a suspended parachute down to the ground. You were then given time to gather your pen and pencils, small diary book, letters and papers, which, snatched by the wheel and the pressure of the fall, had flown from your pockets.

On one of my visits to Coney Island during the "good old days" I was attracted by a crowd responding to a man who, while mingling with everybody, was putting questions to individuals in the group.

"What's your name? Just murmur your name in my ear," the man was saying. Then he printed the given name on a large white card and held it up for people to see. He then asked his blindfolded partner, standing on the platform, what was the name he had printed on the white large card. Invariably and instantly the blindfolded man answered: "The name is Mary." "The name is Peter." "The name is John."

Then the man, still walking among the crowd, came to me and asked the customary question: "What's your name?" "My name is Jesús," I answered in a familiar tone of voice.

"What did you say your name was?"

"My name is Jesús."

"Again?"

"My name is Jesús Colón."

He printed my name on the usual white large card and showed it to everybody.

I showed him my library card, social security card, and personal letters to certify that my name was indeed Jesús.

With the name John, Mary, and Peter the man walking among the crowd just threw the coded phrase words pertaining to those familiar names to his blindfolded partner on the high platform. And—Eureka!—the answer was flashed back to the audience in a matter of seconds. But this time, when he asked my name, a long dialogue back and forth between the blindfolded man and the questioner amused the whole group. The question man was hemming and hawing. His previous rapidity and fluidity of language had been replaced by tongue-tied monosyllables almost inaudible to the rest of those present. The question man was sweating profusely.

When all the rephrasing of the words shouted to the blindfolded man failed to elicit my name from his stuttering lips, the questioner came to me with a "prize." Take this prize and get the hell out of here.

Imagine sending Jesus to hell!

I kept the prize with me for many years. It was a tiny plaster of Paris copy of Rodin's *The Thinker*.

I kept it with me as a reminder that man, as yet, doesn't know everything.

Dalmau

There are many sentimental, thoroughly romantic Puerto Ricans living in the states who think that we have not produced our quota of thieves, jailbirds, perverts, and other characters living in our own underworlds of the big northern cities. The conditions in which we are forced to live, which block the path to better jobs and cleaner neighborhoods, tend to breed these characteristics in any people.

But let us get away from the heavy analysis and get to the story of my friend Dalmau. I never knew his first name, for, as he put it, "We are friends from the streets."

Of this world—the Puerto Rican ghetto of the twenties and thirties in Brooklyn—only those who lived there knew it existed and only a few who cared knew it inside out. Within that ghetto lived thousands of low-paid Puerto Rican workers and church going families.

There for years also lived a group of Puerto Ricans and other Hispanic Americans who spent long hours devising ways and means to live by not working. My friend Dalmau was one of them. I could have been another Dalmau. The only thing that saved me was that I was lucky enough to find in time a political and philosophical ideology through which I channeled my rebellion against the establishment.

I also found among many of those people a decency and a great love for Puerto Rico. You find "real honesty and morality," non-existent in many so-called respectable people.

Dalmau was a thief. He said so himself. But then he added, "I am not an ordinary petty thief that goes into a poor worker's furnished room and steals his Sunday best, to put it into the Bridge Street Pawn Show and then sell the ticket for a few bucks."

"*Yo soy un pillo fino. No soy un ratón.*" ("I am a thief with finesse. I am not a rat.") He finished with a tint of emotion in his voice.

Dalmau was a dresser. On Saturday night, when he started to go dancing and to look for some fun—real fun, he sat for a long time in front of his

49

wardrobe to decide which of the two dozen expensive made-to-order suits he was going to wear.

On some of these Saturday nights, Dalmau used to tell me, "Jesús, why don't you dress in one of my suits—take any one—and go with me to Harlem. Harlem meant 135th Street and Lenox, as there was no large Puerto Rican, Spanish-speaking *Barrio* as yet. "You, working in that Borough Hall Post Office. All kinds of hours for a pittance. Boxing mail ... boxing mail ... monotonous. I would go crazy if I knew I'd have to do that for my whole life. Why don't you live like I live, eh?"

As he paced his two-room apartment on one of the side streets near Myrtle Avenue, he went into high praise of stealing. "What's wrong with stealing? Everybody steals. Some more, some less. But everybody steals. Senators steal, Congressmen steal, bankers steal, cops steal ... ," Dalmau said.

And then he added: "The only difference between those gents and me is that they are seldom caught. They steal in larger quantities. They have mastered the art and science of how not to get caught. And when one gets caught, the others protect him. They belong to a gang, just like us." (He was referring to the little gang of Puerto Ricans and other Latin American thieves on the *Avenida* [Myrtle Avenue]). "And they have power, those big sharks." Then he let out a loud laugh, showing his row of golden teeth. The laugh kept diminishing in volume until it died into a snicker.

A long silence. Then, as if talking to himself again, "If only I had an education ... "

As usual I said, "Until next Saturday, have a good time." He would answer from the top of the stairs, "Keep on reading. Keep on going to night school, Jesús."

At that time, I was going to night school for which I was much admired by Dalmau and others in the group. If any stranger or someone new to the gang tried to mock my passive look, my book under my arm or mockingly tried to snatch my glasses, one of them would leap to my side and with an authoritative glance say, "Let Jesús alone. He wants to be somebody." He would give that last word, an intonation and a meaning I came to interpret as: "If Jesús comes to be something in the future, he might be able to help us in a pinch. He might become a Judge perhaps."

One day, as I was coming from the Carlos Tapia pool room and restaurant on Union Street, I saw Dalmau. He was on the other side of the street surrounded with his usual pack of parasites. Dalmau was smiling. A cigarette or two of marijuana seemed to have placed him in a festive mood. I kept on walking silently and unobtrusively on the other side of the street, doing my best not to be noticed by him. *"No se escabulla, Cabo.¹ No se esconda."* (Don't try to get away, Cabo. Don't hide away from me.) (Cabo was the name which old-time Puerto Ricans in this Brooklyn ghetto used to call each other).

I crossed the street. I made an excuse. "I saw you talking so lively with your group of friends, I didn't want to interrupt," I lied.

"You there, get me a taxi. I want to take Cabo Jesús home." Dalmau didn't listen to my plea. He just demanded my address.

"Where do you live?" "Myrtle Avenue and Waverly," I answered submissively. It was some distance from where he found me. I read in his face that he was preoccupied about something. As we sat, I inquired whether he wanted to take me home or whether he desired to talk on the long ride home about his latest problem.

"Jesús, I have a problem. Drugs have begun to dominate me." He was angry with himself.

"Imagine me, Cabo, letting myself become a slave to a drug." A pause, then ... , "No woman has been able to dominate me. Gambling has been unable to predominate over me; I gamble when I please. The same thing with drinking. Now, what I thought at first to be an insignificant past time ... "

Dalmau knew I couldn't help him. Yet, he wanted a father confessor to whom he could pour out all of his frustrations in combating the growing drug habit. I was accustomed to that role with other persons like Dalmau—men and women.

The taxi arrived at the door of the building where I lived. We stepped out.

"Why don't you come upstairs to meet my mother and the rest of my family?" I asked him more from a sense of courtesy than a sense of desire.

An answer came surprisingly quick from Dalmau's mouth, "Jesús, you know we are friends, very good friends, from the streets and the *Avenida*. But you should also know that Dalmau, a thief, is not 'morally' clean enough to sit in your living room with your family."

Later, I heard that Dalmau was caught by the police for a petty thievery. He was sent to Riker's Island for a year. It seemed that, in order to get the necessary amount of money to sustain his expensive habit, he had to lower his high standards of thieving only in the rich neighborhoods. He had to sell

¹Cabo was the term utilized in the Avenida district of Brooklyn during the 1920s. It meant an old-time Puerto Rican living there for many years. An equal among equals who would never aspire to be a sergeant. A newcomer would never be called a Cabo. He would be, after he was there a number of years. The term spread somewhat to other Puerto Rican neighborhoods of the period.

his fine suits one by one, and all his well-tailored overcoats and shirts, his shoes and ties. His flock of parasitic friends from the old days disappeared.

When Dalmau went to the Island, he was wearing discolored dungarees and a friend's shirt. In his mounting drug habit, he traveled rather fast from marijuana, to cocaine, to heroine. He didn't have any money to buy any of these drugs, all of which were sold inside the prison by some prison guards and other inmates.

His year of confinement got him away from his customary drug pushers. That and some initial treatment from the prison medic, gave him a sense of being cured when he came out. He was a very happy man the day he was released.

The minute the pushers knew that Dalmau was out, they went after him relentlessly. They knew he was a good customer. They offered him drugs on what might be called today a "use now and pay later" plan. Dalmau knew how to get the money.

The pressure was too great and Dalmau's will power had become too weak. The Dalmau of old, the proud fashion plate of the *Avenida* was gone. It had been superseded by a Dalmau of ragged dirty shirts and discolored dungarees.

One sunny morning, Dalmau went into the Lincoln Restaurant. He was not accompanied by any of his coterie of parasites. Nobody sat at the table where he was sitting. He was just a bundle of pestiferous walking rags.

Dalmau asked for a cup of coffee. Nothing more, just a cup of coffee. As he sat with his elbows on the table, he slowly sipped his coffee and stared at the ceiling. Suddenly, it seemed that he had arrived at a decision. Slowly and calmly, he drew a small gun from his ragged dungaree pants. He placed the barrel of the gun inside his own mouth, drew the trigger and blew out his brains.

Angels in My Hometown Church

During my childhood I was very sure that angels existed. That there were white, brown and black angels in a heaven of equality and contentment all its own.

That was in my hometown of Cayey, Puerto Rico, many more years ago than I care to remember.

One of the greatest pleasures was to walk through the silence of the old church, and take long looks at the Virgin Mary painted on the church's walls by our town's immortal Don Ramón Frade.[1]

This great Puerto Rican painter was a man with very peculiar ideas. Don Ramón Frade surrounded the Virgin Mary with a multitude of angels—white, brown and black.

My best childhood friend was Pedro. He lived in one of the few houses that could be called mansions in my hometown. Everybody called Pedro, Pedrito. For, in Puerto Rico, if your name is Pedro and you are poor, they just call you Pedro but if your parents own a mansion with a balcony all around it, then everybody calls you Pedrito.

Pedrito, my childhood friend, was chubby and white. He looked like one of the angels painted around the Virgin Mary. Our favorite playground was the clean piece of land right near his parent's mansion.

So, when Doña María Luisa Martínez de Rodríguez y Acevedo, mother of my best friend Pedrito, shouted to her son from her balcony: "Pedritooooo ... Pedrito ... come over here immediately! You should not be playing in front of the church with ... that boy!"

"But he is my friend!" Pedrito shouted back.

"You should not have a friend of that color! Come over here immediately," Doña María Luisa Martínez de Rodríguez y Acevedo commanded in a tone of finality.

When this happened—and it happened regularly at least once a week during my childhood—I went inside the church and stood for a long time

[1]Puerto Rican painter (1875–1954) from Cayey whose work is mostly characterized by nativist and religious themes.

53

in front of the Virgin Mary's painting on the wall, surrounded with all the white, brown and black angels around her. And I felt good.

Then, in August 1965, my North American wife and I went for a vacation in my hometown in Puerto Rico. "Let's go into the church." My wife looked at me queerly. She knew I have not been much of a church-goer all through the long years of our married life. As we went in, I directed myself, as in my childhood, to the wall in which the Virgin Mary had always been, surrounded by her white, brown and black little angels. The Virgin Mary was still there. She was still surrounded by angels, but all of them were now white. Coats of grey cement covered the space where the brown and black
. . .

I waited until a well-dressed white lady with a fine silken shawl, piously kneeling in front of a Christ figure, got up and finished her praying. Pointing to the Virgin Mary and the few remaining white angels around her, I asked, "Where are the other angels? I mean the brown, the . . . ." The lady with the fine silken shawl didn't let me finish.

"Well, the church had to be painted and remodeled. While taking note of what had to be done, it was noticed that part of the wall in which Don Ramon's Virgin Mary is painted is becoming . . . deteriorated by some rain water infusing through the church roof."

"But how is it that only that part of the painting in which the brown and the . . . ."

"Well, . . . that's the way it was," the lady with the fine shawl interrupted. And then she added, "Those parts became very grimy and they just had to be covered with cement. After a long pause, the lady continued in a very pious and grave tone of voice: "You know Puerto Rico is becoming a great tourist center. Many, many Americans are visiting our hometown and our church every year . . . You have been living in the United States for a very long time . . . Don Ramón Frade, the pride, not only of our hometown but of Puerto Rico, had very queer ideas . . . "

"I know exactly what you are trying to say," I answered curtly, hurriedly walking away from her.

Then, as I came out for air, I thought I heard a voice ricocheting from the church's thick walls that through time and space refused to die. It was the voice of Doña María Luisa Martínez y Acevedo, shouting from her mansion's balcony to her son: "Pedritoooo . . . Pedritoooo . . . Come over here immediately!!! You shouldn't be playing in front of the church with . . . that boy!!!!!"

The Meanest Man in My Hometown

I was there when Pancho Malo was killed. Everybody knew he would be. But when, by whom?

If Pancho Malo was walking toward you in one of the narrow sidewalks of my hometown, with its deep open sewer alongside, you had better jump quickly into the street, for he would push you into the gutter.

Once, a kid was about to start eating a boiled corn-on-the-cob he had just bought from the woman at the marketplace. Pancho snatched it from the boy's hands. Then, with a grin that suddenly exploded into a laugh, Pancho returned the grainless cob to the kid. The kid walked away crying.

Everybody in town predicted Pancho Malo's "accidental" death, because of the lecherous looks he cast at women as they passed by with or without their husbands and because of his habit of plucking the most beautiful flowers in the public gardens on the square and crushing them under his shoes without even smelling them once.

I remember very well the day Pancho Malo was killed. It was the same day the boy from the country usually came to sell his *melcocha* pieces of coconut stuck together with molasses. The mixture was spread thin and set on a long wooden board to harden. Then it was cut in small squares and sold for a penny a piece. As the boy sold his *melcocha*, he lifted each piece with the tip of a long bread knife placed under each candy square.

Rudely elbowing his way to the front of the *melcocha* board, Pancho Malo demanded to be served *pronto*. He had a bunch of pennies in his left hand. As he gulped down a piece of *melcocha*, served right into his big mouth from the tip of the boy's knife, Pancho Malo started piling pennies at one end of the candy board and counted aloud for all to hear: "one ... two ... three ... four ... five ... six ... seven ... eight ... " The pile of brown pennies began to look like the Tower of Pisa. "Nine ... ten ... "

As the boy placed the tenth piece of *melcocha* into the bad man's mouth, Pancho Malo swept the ten pennies from the counter into his right hand. With a quick movement he pocketed them and mockingly began to jingle them in his pocket.

"So you thought I was going to pay you, eh?" Pancho Malo guffawed right into the boy's face. "You know who I am?"

"Pancho MAAALLOOO!" the boy howled as he plunged his *melcocha* knife into Pancho's heart.

It was all very sudden. It took some time before the group around the *melcocha* board realized what had happened. An old lady mumbled something about David and Goliath as she kept crossing herself.

Pancho Malo took a few uncertain steps, trying to keep himself from falling, but everybody backed away from him. Then he fell head first into the dirty, murky waters alongside the sidewalk, the ditch into which he had laughingly pushed so many others.

The dirty, murky waters opened up to receive Pancho's body. They seemed to have been waiting for him for a long time.

The *Fanguito* Is Still There

In our vacation to our native Puerto Rico—"the enchanted island" as described by the tourist trade—we decided to stray from the tourist-trodden path. We wanted to see the other side of the tourist model, the side that lay behind the luxurious hotels and in the least publicized side of the public projects being built supposedly to lodge the families now living in San Juan's *El Fanguito* (the mudhole). *El Fanguito* is the largest of the horrible slums proliferating in all cities and towns of Puerto Rico. The oldest of these slums is called *La Perla* (the pearl), and it is in the oceanside of Old San Juan, in Santurce and Hato Rey. Some of them have acquired picturesque names: *Cantera* (the quarry), Korea, *El Relincho* (the neigh).

My wife and I went to see the slum of *El Caño de Martín Peña* (the Martín Peña Sewer). Clara came, camera in hand, to take some pictures. She wanted to expose the whole thing with an illustrated article when she returned to the States. Clara came to the conclusion that the problem of the slums—and generally the problems of housing and colonialism in Puerto Rico—could only be solved by a socialist form of society under a free and sovereign republic.[1]

The slum *El Caño* was like a design for a hell on earth thrown from nowhere by a crazy drunk planner under the influence of a heavy dose of LSD. It consisted of thousands of half-built shacks facing the quarry, each of them precariously dangling on four rotten stilts sunk into the dirtiest, brownest waters we have ever seen. This quarry water was the accumulated refuse of most of the San Juan sewers. It all merged into an inferno of floating dead dogs, dross, and oddly shaped pieces of excrement dancing out of the seas. This indescribable mass of floating dead matter exuded an odor like that of flesh in its last stages of putrefaction. The air around was sticky, heavy, and sickening. The grayish-black mosquitoes buzzed around like fighting planes, attacking your face and all your body. The fleas begrimed us with the stench of all the litter sent down the drains of all the sinks and

---

[1]Colón's second wife was also a journalist and activist in the National Women's Council of the Communist Party.

lavatories in San Juan. Thousands of tons of waste came through the sewers into the narrow channel named the quarry. A few more tons were added by the thousands of families imperceptibly and slowly dying in the shacks facing the channel.

The other "streets" of *El Caño de Martín Peña* not facing the quarry channel were crammed and crooked, becoming narrower and narrower until both sides of the street converged into one narrow lane. At both sides of the "street," before they became one, there were long rectangular ditches full of stagnant water where sidewalks ought to have been. The water was the recipient of unimaginable substances. These ditches served as tributaries to the long narrow quarry in which all the discards and pestilences of the city met and greeted each other in a pestiferous camaraderie.

To traverse these ditches and reach the sheds—caricature of houses— there were thin soiled pieces of boards. To walk across each of these slippery slabs required the skill of a circus tightrope walker. We took our lives in hand and dared to tread some of these hammock-like slabs to peep inside some of the shacks. Empty beer boxes served as chairs. The wife, husband, and some naked children were eating *marifinga*—a concoction of welfare corn meal boiled in salted water which helped them to starve gradually instead of rapidly.

As we were finding our way out of the labyrinth of dead-end "streets," I asked my wife how she would prefer to die, gradually or rapidly.

Before she answered my question, Clara took a last look at *El Caño de Martín Peña* slum. Thousands of shacks on stilts and in them thousands of human beings slowly starving to death. Tears were flowing from her eyes. I sensed a tone of rage in her voice as she answered my question. Gravely accenting every word, she said: "I prefer to die fighting."

P.S. Years after we came back from Puerto Rico, Clara wrote a book: *Enter Fighting: Today's Women.*

Part II: Other Writings

3: Liga Puertorriqueña e Hispana, Brooklyn Section

The Two United States[1]

There are two United States like there are two Puerto Ricos. On the one hand, the United States of the Ku Klux Klan and the Black Legion with all its villainous followers—the Trojan horse of neofascism in this nation—; on the other, the progressive United States of Wallace and Wilkie: men who from Roosevelt to Browder strove for the unification of the forces of progress and freedom for all, according to their different ways of interpreting progress and freedom.

There are also two Puerto Ricos. The Puerto Rico of the *vendepatrias* (those who sell out their country), a country where nascent capitalism is sharing a common cause with North American absenteeist capitalism, by paying measly salaries to the Puerto Rican proletariat; the Puerto Rico where police underlings massacre people during a demonstration on a Palm Sunday[2] or those who strike claiming for another piece of bread.

There is also another glorious Puerto Rico with a revolutionary tradition: the Puerto Rico of Betances and Albizu Campos, of Ruiz Belvis and Hostos;[3] the Puerto Rico that will someday astonish the world.

The North Americans of the Ku Klux Klan type and Puerto Ricans who sell out their country understand each other very well. They are united, not only among themselves, but their brotherhood extends to levels representing the worst enemies of freedom all over the world. The representatives of

[1]This is a translation of "Los otros Estados Unidos" which appeared in Colón's column "Lo que el pueblo me dice" in *Pueblos Hispanos* (April 17, 1943): 3.

[2]A reference to the 1937 Palm Sunday police attack on a Nationalist Party demonstration held in Ponce, Puerto Rico. This event is known in Puerto Rican history as the Masacre de Ponce (Ponce Massacre).

[3]Ramón Emeterio Betances (1827–1898) was a leader of the Puerto Rican separatist movement against Spanish colonial rule. Forced into exile he directed from abroad the Grito de Lares revolt of 1868. Pedro Albizu Campos (1891–1965) became President of the Puerto Rican Nationalist Party in 1930. He was incarcerated for many years in U.S. prisons for his activities against U.S. domination of Puerto Rico. Segundo Ruiz Belvis (1829–1867) was an abolitionist and separatist advocate against Spanish colonial rule. Eugenio María de Hostos (1839–1903) was an educator, writer and separatist advocate against Spanish colonial rule.

Hitlerism, fascism, and the Spanish *falange*[4] in all countries. The Puerto Rican *vendepatrias*[5] are internationally known and very much aware of the advantages of joining the forces of exploitation, abuse, and oppression of other countries. When they come to the United States, they are well received at the airports by the representatives of the great magnates. They lodge in the best hotels where they are wined and dined, where long conversations take place to deliberate new ways and means of extracting the last drop of energy from the emaciated bodies of the workers and peasants from the colony. The sons and daughters of the exploiters from here and back there on the island go to the same universities where they are members of the same exclusive clubs open only to a particular class of students. Their daughters and sons marry among themselves, and the offspring that come out of these unions do not receive names like Jacinta or Juana, but rather prefer Betty or Jean. There is complete unity and understanding among the exploiters.

But what kind of unity and understanding exists between the exploited here in this country and over there in Puerto Rico? Among those who have to get up every day—Black and white, Protestant and Catholic, Puerto Rican or North American—to sweat in a factory? Do we Hispanics belong as much as we should to the worker unions that allow us to join with our working brothers and sisters from other nationalities residing in the United States and to know and better protect our livelihood? Do we respect or at least know what the International Labor Defense or the International Workers Order are? These powerful organizations composed mainly of North Americans, but which have done so much for Puerto Rico and the Puerto Rican people?

These powerful organizations are the true societies that continue to be guided according to the great and constructively democratic revolutionary traditions of the people of the United States. Let us learn what is not taught in the schools about Thomas Jefferson, Thomas Paine, Elijah Lovejoy,[6] Gene Debs,[7] and many other individuals that this country has produced. Let us learn where, how, and why the celebration of the first of May and International Women's Day originated, days which are known and commemorated by those all over the world who proudly call themselves workers. Let us join together in common cause in the struggles of all of those others who constitute the REAL United States. Let us respect its progressive institutions, its TRUE history and traditions, ranging from the famous words of Patrick Henry to Virginia's colonial legislature to the most recent of Marcantonio's Congressional appearances claiming for justice and liberty on behalf

[4]The pro-Franco supporters during the Spanish Civil War.
[5]Those who sell their country.
[6]Lovejoy was a U.S. socialist labor leader.
[7]Eugene Victor Debs (1855–1926) was a U.S. socialist leader.

of Puerto Rico.

Those of us who are part of the people of Puerto Rico, let us share common cause with the PEOPLE of the United States against the exploiters from both countries.

Only then will we be able to avoid finding ourselves in a concentration camp here or in Puerto Rico four or five years from now, still arguing about whether or not we should stand when the U. S. national anthem is playing.

4: Vanguardia Puertorriqueña, Mother's Day Celebration, 1937

The Jewish People and Us[1]

For most Hispanics a Jew means the landlord, the man who sells dresses and suits on layaway, the exploiting proprietor of the factory where we work together with the "red" or "communist" agitators. The Jew—and this word is always pronounced in a derogatory manner—is the person who sold out Christ. Wasn't this what we were told by the good and wise priest from that orange and pink colored church of our childhood where we learned catechism? Weren't our souls filled with anger and rejoice when during the day before Easter, we would stone and carry all over town a ridiculous stuffed doll tied up and sitting straight on a coalman's horse, yelling "¡El Juá! ¡El Juá!"[2]

As we can see our emotions have been conditioned since childhood to express this scorn and hatred that, when analyzed, serves a very definite purpose. And what is that purpose? Who are the ones interested in promoting scorn and hatred toward the Jew? Let us see.

Under every system of exploitation of man by man—be it a system of barbarism or slavery, feudalism or capitalism—the exploiter needs to find, once in a while, where to displace the blame for poverty, lack of freedoms, and other survival means—conditions in which they have forced the majority of citizens to live. It is necessary to shift this hatred and resentment that the masses would logically express through action against the true oppressors and place the blame, when this understanding comes, and it will, on those truly responsible for having to wage a war every twenty years, for occasionally having to reduce the production of foods and other essential products because there is too much production, while the people die of hunger. The people themselves would take the necessary steps to get rid of the true exploiters, and, for the benefit of the majority, change the present social system.

[1] This is a translation of "Mi mujer no trabaja," written for the workers' newspaper *Oye, boricua*. There is no evidence to date that it was ever published. The original manuscript was among Colón's papers.

[2] A shortened form of "Judas," the betrayer of Christ.

Hitler made a new important contribution to the exploiters. He made hatred against Jews into a science. He systematized and revived all the prejudices and all the historical and scientific mistakes against this race. He made professors and academics of those who, because of money or fear, prostituted science and thought, and promoted through their "treatises" the most discredited falsehoods. He constructed the most perfect propaganda machine, spreading it to every corner of the world into all languages. And through all means, Dr. Goebbels[3] and his satellites presented through a diversity of pseudoscientific articles and speeches a "theory" about the inferiority of certain races, about the unquestionable superiority of the German race over all others, and about the Jew as the cause of all evil.

We the Hispanic people, as an exploited minority group, should not fall into the trap that the exploiters have laid for us to divide the oppressed people among themselves. When we vilify a Jew, who most of the times is just another poor soul who, like most of us, has to sweat for his daily bread, we are sharing common cause with the Hitlers and Goebbels. There are bad and exploiting Jews, we know that. Just like in our own countries and even in our colony, which is mostly proletarian, there are also Hispanics who are evil and exploiters.

We cannot make those Jewish people who have been exploited like us pay for the refugee who was able to purchase his escape from Germany and who never belonged to the exploited class. Let us not help Hitler and all his proselytizing lackeys who are trying to make the Jew the scapegoat of this war and of the . . .

We have grown. Our minds have matured. Let us not continue yelling like children "El Juá! El Juá!" and throwing stones at a silent and hollow doll that has done nothing to us.

Let us direct our anger toward the true enemy of the oppressed. You know who they are. They have neither a country nor a flag.

[3] Adolf Hitler's Minister of Propaganda.

My Wife Doesn't Work[1]

"My wife doesn't work." You don't know how many times I have heard these words from the lips of many married men! They pronounce these words with a certain little proudness like they were doing their wives a favor.

And what is the truth behind the resounding phrase, "My wife doesn't work"? The truth is that the woman who stays home doing house chores works as hard and many times harder than the man that goes out to work.

The saddest thing about all of this is that women's housework is hard to see or remains unacknowledged or unappreciated.

Women's work in the home never ends. There is no clock to punch in the house from the moment a woman begins to prepare breakfast or dress the kids for school, up to the time when she does the dishes and ends the day.

If the baby wakes up and cries in the middle of the night and preparation of a quick bottle is urgently needed to make the child go back to sleep, our average man continues sleeping to his heart content. He doesn't get up, not even to rock the cradle, while the woman is in the kitchen warming up the milk.

The average man comes home from work, sits on a chair in front of the TV and takes his shoes off. With a few sweet words of endearment (*mi negrita, mi amor, mi nena linda*), he asks his wife to fetch his slippers and a cold beer from the refrigerator. When the woman yells, "Dinner is on the table," the man gets up from his chair, washes his hands and sits himself at the table to be served.

Washing dishes after dinner ... That is left up to American husbands!

Afterwards the average man changes his clothes and goes out for a "*vueltecita*" (a little outing) with his buddies. And the woman, who the man says doesn't work, stays home picking up dirty laundry for the wash, imagining

[1]Translation of "Mi mujer no trabaja," written for the workers' newspaper *Oye, Boricua*, but unpublished.

ways of stretching the buck so she can buy more at the *bodega*, or watching one of those never-ending soap operas.

And thus, with the tiny phrase "My wife doesn't work," the average man makes a little slave of the woman, one who serves him twelve to fourteen hours a day without a salary and many times without love. There are some exceptions, but through my own experience I have encountered few.

I am very much afraid that what these kind of men truly mean when they say "My wife doesn't work" is "I don't want my wife to work outside the home because other women at the office or the factory can spoil her." (These men always emphasize the term *mi mujer* as if she were a thing or they would own her in body and soul). "Spoil" in the sense that the average man uses this word, meaning that she would be influenced and learn about her rights as a woman and worker. The day will come when a woman may be able to make more money than her weekly allowance, which would be a mortal blow to masculine claims of superiority.

And who knows if, with the passing of time, that woman begins to read a newspaper like this, that represents her class—the working class. And from then on ... anything goes!

Bitter Sugar: Why Puerto Ricans Leave Home[1]

I still remember the day my teacher in San Juan gave me that fat history book: *A History of the United States.* It was around 1915. I was in the eighth grade, elementary school. I looked curiously at the maps and pictures, and for the first time looked at the oval face of George Washington and the Christlike figure of Abraham Lincoln.

Thumbing through the book, I chanced upon a phrase in one of the documents reproduced at the end of the book. The phrase was: *"We, the people of the United States ... "* The phrase somehow evoked a picture of all those people about whom we had been studying in our flat, cream-colored geography book. The people who picked cotton in Alabama, raised wheat in the Dakotas, and grew grapes in California. The people in the big, far-away American cities who manufactured my mother's Singer machine and the shoes we saw on sale. The people in Brooklyn and other shipyards who built the great big ships that plied the waters of the Caribbean. All these people and I, and my father and the poor Puerto Rican sugar workers and tobacco workers, we were, all together, *"the people of the United States."* We all belonged! That is what the words meant to me, a little schoolboy in Spanish-speaking Puerto Rico, colony of the United States.

My eighth-grade teacher was a six-foot Montanan, Mr. Whole, by name. He was very friendly. There was always a fading smile on his lips. One day he was sitting on the wide porch of the Y.M.C.A. All of us in school had been politely obliged to bring in a quarter each as a contribution for the construction of the building. Mr. Whole hailed me from the porch and invited me to play a game of checkers. I sat in front of him, with the checkerboard between us. Somebody in authority came out and told Mr. Whole that I could not play there with him because I did not belong to the white race.

[1]Originally published in *Fraternal Outlook* 10.1 (1948): 18-19. A version of this essay was later published in *A Puerto Rican in New York and Other Sketches* (New York: Masses and Mainstream, 1961) under the title "A Puerto Rican in New York."

That incident started me thinking. In this "we the people" phrase that I admired so much, were there first and second class people? Were there other distinctions and classifications based not only on "race" but on money or social position?

Life and reading gave me the answer. Yes, there were classifications and divisions. The rich and the poor. The sugar planter and the sugar peon. And I soon discovered that the rich Puerto Rican sugar planter and the rich American investor belonged to the same clubs and played golf and danced and dined together. Both despised and exploited the masses of the Puerto Rican people.

I learned that the Americans did not come to Puerto Rico because of the altruistic and democratic reasons that General Miles[2] had stated in his famous proclamation when the Yankees invaded Puerto Rico in 1898. I learned that a race to gain control of the resources and the markets of the world was then going on. The United States was first getting into this race in earnest around 1898. I learned the meaning of the word imperialism. I further learned that ever since the Americans had come into Puerto Rico, our country, which had produced the varied products for our daily meals, was converted into a huge sugar factory with absentee owners caring absolutely nothing about the standards of living of the agricultural workers who comprise two-thirds of the Puerto Rican population. A man's sunrise to sunset labor under the burning tropical sun, cutting sugar cane, yielded one dollar and a half a day.

I realized more clearly than before that all our school books, except our Spanish grammar, were written in English. It would be just as if you New Yorkers or Pennsylvanians discovered one good morning that your children's school books were all written in German or Japanese.

In 1917, there was a big strike of the dock workers. The police were ordered to patrol with long range rifles. Right in front of the school in Puerta de Tierra some of the strikers were marching. It was during the noon recess hour. The mounted police charged them. The dock workers and the Puerta de Tierra women—famous for their militancy—stood firm.

The workers were mauled down by the police. One was killed, many were wounded.

During my first year of high school, I was told by the workers that this legalized murder was nothing new. In the sugar plantations the owners used to burn a stretch of planted sugar cane, impute the arson to the workers and kill them like malaria mosquitoes.

The workers and the course of my life kept teaching me. The workers

[2]Nelson Miles was in charge of the U.S. military forces that invaded Puerto Rico on July 25, 1898.

told me that we were a colony. A sort of storage house for cheap labor and a market for second-class industrial goods. That we Puerto Ricans were a part of a vast colonial system, and that not until colonialism was wiped out and full independence achieved by Puerto Rico would the condition by which we were living be remedied.

Colonialism made me get out of Puerto Rico thirty years ago. Colonialism, with its agricultural slavery, monoculture, absenteeism and rank human exploitation are making the young Puerto Ricans of today come in floods to the United States.

I didn't find any bed of roses in the United States. I found poor pay, long hours, terrible working conditions. I met discrimination even in the slums and in the low-paying factories where the bosses very dexterously pitted Italians against Puerto Ricans, and Puerto Ricans against American Negroes and Jews.

The same American trusts that milked us in Puerto Rico were in control in New York. And the trusts—the fountainhead of imperialism and colonialism, the meaning of which I had learned the hard way—were not only oppressing the Puerto Ricans in New York, but the other various national minorities and workers as well.

Today there are approximately 400,000 Puerto Ricans in greater New York. The largest number live in East Harlem, from 98th to ll6th Street, between 5th and Lexington Avenues. Then comes the second largest Puerto Rican community, around Longwood and Prospect Avenues in the Bronx. The third largest concentration is around the Williamsburg section in Brooklyn. There are smaller Puerto Rican communities from Bay Ridge in Brooklyn to Yonkers.

Why have the reactionary newspapers unleashed a concerted campaign against the Puerto Ricans coming to New York? Why do they describe the Puerto Ricans in the worst light they can imagine? Simply because they know that colonial conditions of exploitation and the cry for their economic, social and political independence have made the Puerto Ricans a freedom-loving democratic people. Their American idol is Vito Marcantonio.[3] Because they are progressives with the right to vote as American citizens, the reactionaries hate them and are trying to intimidate them and frighten them into submission.

The Puerto Ricans are joining the unions and the progressive fraternal, civic and political organizations. They are looking for and achieving unity with the other national groups and progressive forces in America today.

---

[3]Italian American Congressman from New York active in the Puerto Rican community.

Increasing numbers are joining the Cervantes Society of the I.W.O.[4]

The Puerto Ricans now arriving are learning the power of unity. At the call of Representative Vito Marcantonio, a broad organization of all Puerto Ricans has been established after two great conferences of representatives from fraternal, religious, civic and political organizations. This Convention for Puerto Rico, as the organization is called, has as its main purpose the ending of the colonial status of Puerto Rico and achievement of the civil rights of the Puerto Ricans in this country.

[4]Colón was president of this society which was part of the International Workers' Order.

Mueren 42 Al Caer Avión En Golfo De México

(INFORMACION EN PAGINA 2)

TIEMPO: NUBLADO
Temperatura Máxima
50 Grados

EL DIARIO
DE NUEVA YORK

7 cts.
Mayor Circulación
Diaria en los E. U.

VOL. XII   144 Duane Street New York 13, N. Y.   NUEVA YORK — MARTES, 17 DE NOVIEMBRE DE 1959.   Second Class Postage Paid at New York, N. Y.   NO. 3,656

Ante Comité Cameral

Identifican Boricua Como Líder Rojo NY

IDENTIFICACION POSITIVA. — La detective Mildred Blauvelt (de pie, a la derecha) señala hacia Jesús Colón para identificarlo como líder rojo, mientras éste declaraba ayer ante el Comité de Actividades Anti-Americanas de la Cámara Federal que investiga las actividades del Partido Comunista en la comunidad puertorriqueña e hispana en Nueva York. Colón y otro testigo, identificado como Félix Ojeda Ruiz, rehusaron responder a las preguntas que les fueron formuladas, cobijándose en la Quinta Enmienda Constitucional. — (Inf. en la Pág. 2)
(Foto: EL DIARIO).

5: Front page of *El Diario de Nueva York*, November 17, 1959

Pilgrimage of Prayer[1]

From nine thousand churches all over this land, from thousands of trade unions halls, community centers, social clubs, fraternal lodges, organized blocks and ad hoc committees, from homes with people of all colors and all creeds, in hamlets and in cities, north, south, east and west, the pilgrims will walk, drive, fly and go by train to Washington, capitol of the United States.

Why are they going? Simple enough: to raise their voices in prayer. Prayer? Yes, just prayer.

The date: Friday May 17, 1957. The place: in front of the Lincoln Memorial. The time: high noon.

To think that American Negro and white children will be reciting this date in future history classes all over this land when the teacher asks them.

"When?"

And they will answer: May 17, 1957.

"Where?"

At the Lincoln Memorial in Washington.

"Why?"

"To pray"

And I am sure that at a future history class the teacher will go into details about what they were praying for, why thousands of men, women and children traveled thousands of miles to be together, seventy-five thousand of them, to raise their voices in prayer.

What will they pray for? They are going to pray to demonstrate their determination to achieve first class citizenship, to invite Northerners to act in common on a great issue with the Southern Freedom Fighters. In their praying they are going to protest the curtailment of the NAACP and attempts of the Southern bigots to outlaw that organization in the South. They are going to protest "violence directed at those in the South who assert their dignity and stand up for equality and freedom." They are going to "press

[1]Published in *The Daily Worker* (May 14, 1957).

74

for civil rights legislation before Congress which, for the first time since Reconstruction days, has a chance to be enacted." All these aims are embodied in the five-point objectives of this pilgrimage.

While these thousands of Negro and white pilgrims are traveling over the highways and airways of this nation in their efforts to reach the capitol by May 17 noon, life will continue to travel with them. They will see things, they will listen, they will learn many new things and add many experiences to their thoughts and feelings. And the objectives of the pilgrimage will grow in depth and clarity and decision because of the multiple experiences of every individual participating, as they journey to and from Washington and as they take part in the very act of praying at the capitol itself. Not one will be the same after he or she gets back from the pilgrimage. You will not notice it right away, but something will have been added. But all those "somethings" added to all of us summed up will represent a collective force for good and for action that could not be easily measured or estimated in its immediate effects. Imagine the mental processes in the minds of the government big wheels as they watch from their office widows, humanity pouring into the surroundings of the Lincoln Memorial! And oppressed and discriminated, colored and white humanity of all colonies and of all countries will be walking with them. You will almost be able to feel it.

We urge all Spaniards, all Puerto Ricans and all other Spanish-speaking people who can, to join the pilgrimage to Washington, Friday, May 17. By being there you will be helping yourself and your own people. For the achievement of first class citizenship, civil rights and equality of opportunity for the Negro people will mean the achievement of all these rights for all of us.

If you or your friend have an automobile, try to get half a dozen people to go together by auto. Or just to Penn Station at 7:30 on the morning of May 17. Ask for and get on the "Freedom Special!." The round-trip fare on this train will be $9.95. Many churches and neighborhoods and other organizations in the neighborhoods are chartering buses. Inquire. The bus fare should be around $5.50 to $6.00 round-trip. For further information write to the "Prayer Pilgrimage for Freedom," 217 W. 125 St., N.Y.C. Or call MO–6–6997.

Let us all go to Washington, Negro, white and brown. Let us be there in order to help the United States be the kind of democracy—not in theory but in fact—that we all want it to be.

Over three hundred years ago, the pilgrims came to the coast of New England. They came in protest against the violations of their material and spiritual rights by the rulers of England. They also dedicated prayers. When they were not praying they were clearing the land, tilling the soil and building roads and towns. They took time out to discuss and write the "Mayflower Compact." Their descendants and many others who came later wrote the Declaration of Independence, the Constitution with the Bill of Rights. In the country's development grave and great injustices and crimes were committed against the Indians, the Negro slaves and the white-exploited workers. It is true that these injustices are still taking place. It is also true that great battles for freedoms never heard of in the Europe of those days were fought for and won. Sometimes we tend to forget the positive side of this nation's history. It is also true that a well-heeled minority class usurped or bought the public, military and economic power, converting this nation into the greatest imperialist government in the world.

It is about time to begin to study how this happened—not in slogans but in detail—, how the people's power was taken away from the people. For still the Mayflower Compact is there, the Declaration of Independence is there, the Constitution with its Bill of Rights and the battered Fifth is there. And when seventy-five thousand people congregate to pray at the Lincoln Memorial this coming Friday, they will walk into the Memorial and read on its South Wall Lincoln's immortal words at Gettysburg:

FOUR SCORE AND SEVEN YEARS AGO OUR FATHERS BROUGHT FORTH ON THIS CONTINENT A NEW NA-TION CONCEIVED IN LIBERTY AND DEDICATED TO THE PROPOSITION THAT ALL MEN ARE CREATED EQUAL

It is for us the plain people to restore the hallowed documents to their daily use and application and put all segregation and all other anti-peoples laws in the wastebasket of history.

A great chapter in the history of the United States started with a prayer at Plymouth Rock. It might well be that another great chapter in the history of this country might also start with a prayer at the Lincoln Memorial this coming Friday at high noon.

Phrase Heard in a Bus[1]

Many years ago—almost forty—I had an argument with a conductor on a Fifth Ave. bus, one of the old double-decker Fifth Ave. busses. In those days long, long ago I loved to leave my drab, unheated room in Brooklyn to get "lost" in the strange neighborhoods of the big city. I liked to find for myself the "cities" within the big city and would go through them, observing the strange people and the houses, peering into store windows, with their little known merchandise brought here from the four corners of the earth. One day, forty years ago, my wanderings took me to Washington Square. In those days Washington Square was more Washington Square than it is today. The Square has been losing its distinct personality during these last few years.

After walking around the Square for a while in my youthful curiosity, I decided to take a ride in one of those queer looking double-decker busses with the curved stairs to the top sight-seeing part.

I seated myself on the very front seat of the top part. As the bus started up Fifth Ave., passing the stately mansions right and left, the conductor came with his little piggy bank that gave a timid clinking sound as the nickel was inserted into it. The conductor took a long look at me sitting in the front seat of the upper level. After getting my nickel and examining me from head to foot, he solemnly informed me that "my place" was down below, that I was not supposed to sit in the upper sight-seeing seats.

Does this sound incredible—my young reader of 1957? How many of those "little" things were "pulled" against you if you were a Negro in those days forty years ago! How many of these "little" incredible things, my young reader, are "pulled" today against Negroes and Puerto Ricans even as I am writing these lines!

Well, I guess, I don't have to tell you that I did not budge from my front seat on the upper sight-seeing part of that bus. I vaguely suspected that, even at that time many years ago when I did not really understand a thing or two

[1]Published in *The Daily Worker* (July 2, 1957).

77

as clearly as I understand them now, my color had something to do with the strange conduct on the Fifth Ave. bus conductor.

Ever since that incident forty years ago, I have been more or less prejudiced against the Fifth Ave. busses. Against the uppity attitude of many of the people riding them, especially those who ride and live within Washington Square and the eighties; after 80th Street the bus seems to become humanized again by the predominance of the domestic and other kinds of workers riding to their homes in the working-class districts of the city.

Again, let us avoid sweeping characterizations. I am sure that within those high rent apartments that now occupy the sites of the stately old mansions there must be quite a number of humane, sensitive people ... But still, even today with the flat one floor busses replacing the aristocratic looking old ones, there is an air of upper class artificiality, a sort of artificial chitchat of the ladies commenting on their goings and comings to Paris and Bermuda said audibly enough to be heard by those seated nearby while riding on the "vulgar" bus. I don't have to tell you that this kind of "conversation" usually heard on the Fifth Ave. bus between the Square and the 59th and the eighties is far different from the talk heard on the Fourth or Eight Ave. busses. Again, I repeat, I might be a little prejudiced because of what happened to me on one of those busses forty years ago.

About a week ago I took the Fifth Ave. bus on 12th St. and Fifth Ave. I sat in an empty seat in back of two bejeweled, perfumed, expensively dressed ladies who were probably residents of lower Fifth Ave. You could not help but listen to their conversation, as it was conducted in a pitch high above all the compounded noises on the avenue and in the bus. It seemed that the two ladies wanted everybody to know how many charities they had sponsored and how many benefit balls they had a hand in organizing during the winter for this, that and the other worthy cause. It seemed to me that these two ladies were having a lot of fun while throwing crumbs of charity to the needy and the disabled of society.

As one of the ladies started to comment about her coming charitable summer activities, she informed everybody in the bus, while seemingly speaking solely to her companion, "Why, take this boat ride for the poor children and their mothers ... It will create a great inconvenience for me. As one of the active persons in the committee I will have to be present at the Battery at least until the boat leaves for Bear Mountain. Still, at that very hour on that Sunday I would like to be at a very important private social affair which I would like very much to attend." And then arranging her lady-like coiffure with both her white, long-gloved hands, she added coldly and insensitively, "Oh, I hope that Sunday it will rain cats and dogs so that the boat ride will have to be canceled and I can attend that affair."

Those last words hit me like a thunderbolt. Yet they were said, so calmly, so serenely, yet so seriously. They were not said as a joke, but as a prayer. I looked fixedly at her bejeweled neck, at her perfumed shoulders, at her brocaded back and I saw a callous human being loose in the jungle of "civilized society." That the hundreds of mothers and children that will have to stay cooped in their small slum apartments if it rained "cats and dogs" that Sunday did not seem to bother her at all. That the hundreds of home-made sandwiches and jugs of lemonades tucked in old shopping bags and carried by the family kids with mouth-watered anticipation did not mean a thing to this perfumed beast. That this boat ride would constitute THE summer and will be THE talk all through the coming long winter evenings at the neighbor's flat did not seem to strike her imagination in the least. The months of waiting and preparation and pinching of pennies for the expenses of the boat ride since the day the families received their tickets from her charity committees was nothing at all for this ... lady.

I was glad when she got off with her companion around 34th St. and Fifth Ave.

Which should remind us that when, we the people, take full political and economic power, the job will have just begun. It will take years after the people take power to develop a human being without the callousness and insensitivity wrought into millions of men and women by the low morals of capitalism. Even after years when socialism will seem to be well rooted in our land—and there is no doubt that this will come to pass—our grandchildren will still be discovering among themselves some of the tenets of the evil thinking and acting of the so-called civilized society of today.

Little Rock[1]

Little Rock has become a big rock thrown at the American show window where the boasted articles of equality and democracy for all has been displayed for years as enticing objects for the colonial and all colored peoples of the world.

We have no doubt that this Little Rock has opened the head of many, including Negroes and whites. They include those who have been telling us that something like what is happening in Little Rock cannot happen in this day and age in the United States. These illusioned ones have been awakened, alerted and reeducated to the fundamental fact that basically, in all these years of nibbling at the problem and giving small concessions from Booker T. Washington's[2] time to the weak Civil Rights Bill just passed by the last Congress, the question of FULL equality to the negro people has not changed.

This is the main objective that we have to keep in mind at all times.

Do we mean that we are to deny the existence of the rights won in the Civil War and after? That we are to cross out as inadequate the latest watered federal Civil Rights law? Not at all. WE are to keep fighting for more of these concessions and reforms. All that we ought not to forget is that all these concessions and reforms have been gotten and are being won by the struggle of a Negro and progressive white minority against a white racial resistance based on ignorance of many years standing. In short, we should not forget, looking at the gains, that the basic admission that Negroes ought to have the same rights and privileges as anybody else is not yet recognized flatly and in life without any ifs or buts by the majority of the white population that has been poisoned for years by those capitalist interests who thrive and profit by this policy of divide and conquer.

[1]Published in *The Daily Worker* (October 8, 1957).
[2]Booker T. Washington (1856–1915) was an African American educator. He is the author of *Up from Slavery* (1901) and *The Story of the Negro* (1909).

We progressives of all races have been as yet unable to win the wide masses of white people, especially in the South, from this poison of chauvinism that keeps the working class and the people in general weak and divided. This is still the sad objective fact.

When you are blinded by the position won today by a Dr. Bunche or by a couple of Negro cadets graduating from West Point and forget that the predominant trend inculcated by all the tools in the hands of capitalist racial bias among the white population, then you are abandoning objective reality and entering the camp of illusion and wishful thinking.

That is why we—Negro, white, Indians, Chinese, Puerto Ricans or what-have you—who have liberated (or thought we have liberated) ourselves from racial prejudices have a tremendous job to accomplish. And be it said right here that there are more whites freed from racial prejudice than many of the extremists in all races happen to think there are.

First of all, we have to examine and reexamine ourselves and our attitudes and daily relations with other races. This should be an everyday examination. The atmosphere is so thick with chauvinism and all kinds of national and racial prejudice of every sort that we are not exaggerating when we recommend such a continuous and thorough checkup.

When the statement in the Declaration of Independence that "all men are created equal" comes to be looked upon as a rhetorical phrase to be mechanically parroted at commencement time or on the 4th of July, then anything is liable to happen when it comes to race relations.

But the most tragic thing of all is that aside from all this race prejudice—race hate in many instances—many of these people are normal persons. That is why we say again that the Negro and white who have managed to get rid of prejudice in the main have a tremendous job to do. The job is difficult and complicated. It cannot be done by just thinking that you can exorcise chauvinism from people by ridiculing, insulting, howling and calling them ignorant. By this method of insult and innuendo all that we can achieve is to alienate those who are just getting rid of the capitalist poison. We need all the recruits we can get, regardless of their color, in this collective raceless fight for true American equality and democracy. Sometimes the most sublime causes are strangled by those who claim to love and defend the west.

Our immediate task seems to be to convince those who are for the admittance of the Negro children because "it is the law" to the position that the Negro children should be admitted because it is the just, the proper, the right, the civilized thing to do. Just as there are those who still reserve their "right" to be prejudiced behind the phrase, "It is the law," there are others who keep their prejudices behind other phrases or "practical solutions" to the Negro question. Not until we get rid of all the "moral," "practical" props on this question and accept the Negro and the members of all other colored races as equal not only "before the law" but anywhere else, can we say that we are getting rid of chauvinism and racial and national prejudices in this nation.

Only then might we start to regain the respect that Little Rock and all that came before had made us lose among the colonial people and all the nations and peoples of the world.

Let us also guard ourselves against a sort of formalism on this question. To write and unanimously approve a resolution against "the reactionary forces" in Little Rock is good. To approve a sum of money—big and small—from the treasury of our organization to help fight racial discrimination is also good. But it seems to me that we ought to try to do something beyond passing resolutions or assigning a sum of money, good as these things may be. We OURSELVES ought to do something individually and collectively on this first point in the agenda of the problems in the United States today. Had I more space, I would tell you what we did in a place where I used to work and where some symptoms of race prejudice began to be noticed.

I tell you what a friend of mine did about Little Rock in the factory where he works. We will call him Joe. A day or so after Phallus[3] barred the doors of the Central High School to the Negro children, Joe took a rough piece of paper from the factory and wrote a request to the President of the United States to use his federal and military powers to keep open the doors of the high school to the Negro children. Joe then asked the sixty workers in his shop to sign their names to the request. About forty of them signed. The whole question was thoroughly discussed by the workers. Then Joe put the whole thing in an envelope and sent it to President Eisenhower. Joe is a white worker. Can you imagine the effect in the White House if other Joes in thousands of other factories and offices all over the nation would have done the same? Enough said.

[3]A disparaging reference to Orval E. Faubus, Governor of Alabama, who on September 1957, the eve of the full-scale integration of the public schools mandated by the Federal government, called out the National Guard supposedly to "maintain order." As a result nine African-American children were barred from attending Central High School on opening day.

6: Jesús Colón, 1960s

A Growing Minority[1]

I remember when we had just one Puerto Rican grocery store, one Puerto Rican restaurant and one such barbershop in all of New York City. No matter where you lived you had to take the old nickel IRT to 145th St. and Madison Ave. if you wanted a haircut in a Puerto Rican barbershop so you would not be discriminated against because of race, color, nationality or accent.

That was more than forty years ago. Today over half a million Puerto Ricans live in greater New York alone. Statistics say that we will be one solid million in this city by 1960.

There are also substantial Puerto Rican communities in almost every major northern U. S. city. In the South, with the exception of Miami and several seasonal labor camps in Florida, there are no noticeable Puerto Rican communities.

Contrary to common opinion, wherever the Puerto Rican goes he tries to organize himself into some sort of a group or a society. That many of these societies are not what their constitutions and bylaws say they are is very true. This gives part of the Puerto Rican residents a sort of what's the use outlook on joining organizations. To the superficial observer this looks as if it might be the outlook of all Puerto Ricans. This Puerto Rican is a very sociable person who likes to join and cooperate when the aims of a movement make sense to him.

It would be interesting to make a nationwide study of how the Puerto Rican is faring in the various sections of this nation.

When a delegation representing Puerto Rican communities of Manhattan, Bronx, Brooklyn, Queens, Middletown, Buffalo and Rochester went to Albany to back the Metcal-Baker bill prohibiting discrimination in housing, in the entire state as the Sharkey-Brown-Isaacs bill, effective April 1, will for this city, state senators and assemblymen went out of the way to participate. This reflected the change in the last ten or fifteen years in the power of the Puerto Rican vote potential.

[1]Published in *The Worker* (March 30, 1958).

Facing discrimination in the town of Dunkirk near Buffalo, the Puerto Ricans there organized the Puerto Rican American Organization, an action sparked by the illegal search of the Ramón Vargas Correa home. Vargas Correa is a popular and active Puerto Rican in Dunkirk.

In Connecticut, especially in New Haven and Hartford, the Puerto Ricans are numerous, and becoming increasingly conscious of their political strength. Their voice is beginning to be heard by both major parties. There is little independent political thought as yet among these Puerto Ricans. A Puerto Rican monthly was published, but it never came out regularly.

In New Jersey, especially in Newark and Hoboken, the Puerto Ricans have quite a number of political and social clubs. Gov. Robert Meyner recently thought it the proper thing to do to visit Puerto Rico. He has given audiences to Puerto Rican delegations bringing grievances.

It could be said that the prompt removal of Judge Frank Lloyd, who slandered the Puerto Rican from a high seat in the New Jersey Supreme Court, marked political recognition of Puerto Ricans.

Let me hasten to point out that all these mini-victories are nothing "revolutionary," nothing to change the world tomorrow morning. All that we are saying is that the conditions are being planted in which the Puerto Rican communities will be able, some time in the future, to move into really progressive action if we learn to work with people who do not necessarily agree with us in all points in the political map.

One thing is certain and that is that the Puerto Rican national minority is here to stay.

The Muñoz Marín[2] government has about eleven offices throughout the U. S. whose job it is in part to take care of the organization of the Puerto Ricans for their own particular purpose. In organizing them the Puerto Rican government has in mind a national scope instead of a reduced scope of just one city or one state.

And so, if we are to think in terms of organizing Puerto Ricans in a way that they will eventually be part of the progressive political currents, we have to study them, their organizations and their leadership from a national point of view.

---

[2]Luis Muñoz Marín (1898–1980) was the first governor of Puerto Rico elected by popular vote in 1948. He served in that post until 1964. He was the leading force behind the establishment of the Estado Libre Asociado (Commonwealth) and the Operation Bootstrap industrialization program.

Colonial Showplace[1]

Puerto Rico, or as it is called today, the "Commonwealth of Puerto Rico," is not an independent country. Not all of the legalistic juggling in the U. S. Congress, or its counterpart in Puerto Rico, can hide the fact that Puerto Rico is still a colony of the U. S.

That this colony is assigned the role of being a showcase for other colonial and semicolonial countries cannot obscure the fact that Puerto Rico is still a colony though it presents a seemingly prosperous look for the moment.

That we need a rounded-out Marxist study of this historical moment in Puerto Rican history, from 1938 to 1958—with all of its half-truths and contradictions—, is not denied by anybody. But to confuse the present Keynesian New Capitalism, operation XYZ, experiences and experimentation with a basic solution for Puerto Rico is to believe in miracles.

Certainly these use some positive elements in the present enthusiastic hodge-podge of economic theories and experiments. If it were not so, the showcase would not have any value to American imperialism as a bait for other colonies.

Thousands of U. S. tourists visit Puerto Rico beginning about this time of the year. They return with the following tales, on the strength of their two-week guided bus tour, to prove that the "Commonwealth of Puerto Rico" is free and independent.

We will quote some points raised in a manifesto published by the "Gran Oriente Nacional" masonic lodge of Puerto Rico, of which Dr. Antonio Santaella Blanco is the Grand Master. This document has been widely distributed and was even read in some congresses of important Latin American nations.

Part of the Puerto Rican masonic manifesto reads: "We are a colony because: a) We are citizens of the United States. To Washington there is no such thing as being a citizen of Puerto Rico. American citizenship was

[1]Published in *The Worker*, October 11, 1959): 9.

imposed on us in 1917. As a result of this imposition, our youth had to serve in the Army of the United States during the First World War. We Puerto Ricans must travel with U. S. passports, as there is no Puerto Rican nation, according to our 'good friends' and tutors in Washington. b) Our customs houses are not our own. They belong to the U. S. c) Our currency is not our own. It belongs to the U. S. d) Our Post Offices are not our own. They belong to the U. S. e) The U. S. military service is imposed on Puerto Ricans. It has caused thousands of deaths to our youths during the last three wars 'fighting for democracy' and 'for the rights of nations to liberty and freedom.' Our sons are forced to serve in the U. S. Army when they reach eighteen. If not, U. S. courts, not Puerto Rican courts, judge them, and they are sent to serve time in U. S. prisons. f) Sugar, our most important industry, is controlled by the U. S. We produce 1,300,000 tons of sugar a year. We are only permitted to refine 126,000 tons a year in Puerto Rico. g) Our communications system is equally controlled by Washington. We cannot install a single radio or television station in Puerto Rico without a license previously extended by the authorities in Washington D.C. No short wave stations are permitted. h) The U. S. coastwise shipping laws are also the shipping laws of Puerto Rico. We cannot ship any goods to Puerto Rico or out of Puerto Rico in ships that do not belong to a U. S. shipping company. The United States ship freight charges are the highest in the world. It costs more to send a bag of rice from New York to Puerto Rico in a U. S. ship than from New York to the Argentine Republic in a foreign ship, though the distance is seven times as long. i) The decisions of the Supreme Court of Puerto Rico can be appealed to the Boston Circuit Court of Appeals in the U. S. From there it can be appealed to the U. S. Supreme Court in Washington. j) Puerto Rico is forced to sell all of its products and buy all it consumes in the most expensive market in the world: the U. S. (For 1955–1956, Puerto Rico bought $568,000,000 in goods from the U. S. and sold $389,000,000 to the U. S. This produced a balance against the Puerto Rican economy of $179,000,000). k) The oath of allegiance to the flag and the constitution of the United States of North America is an indispensable requirement for holding office in the city or insular government of Puerto Rico."

It is significant that such an organization of Puerto Ricans as the national "Gran Oriente" of Puerto Rico, composed of supposedly level-headed members, mostly of the well-to-do class, is today advocating independence for Puerto Rico in a manifesto to all Latin American countries.

Let us not be blinded by a Puerto Rican economy based on a tax-free chance for U. S. industrialists to convert Puerto Rico into a sweatshop, airconditioned though it be, of low wages and colonial exploitation.

The Meaning of Algebra[1]

We will say, for the record, that what I am going to tell you happened in Brooklyn, where of course, it did not happen at all.

It was not in Brooklyn that I met this lad. It was in a bus in ... But why specify the borough? It might not be too good for the boy.

As he came into the bus I noticed all the books he was carrying with him. Five books and a well-worn copy of a magazine on space travel.

The boy was cleanly but poorly dressed. He was wearing glasses. He had a winning smile.

He sat down next to me.

"My, how many books! Do you read them all?" I inquired.

"Yep, I read them all," he answered with a tone of assurance.

"You are coming from the public library, aren't you? What do you want to be in life?"

"I want to be an engineer."

The lad talked as if he meant business. As if nobody was going to stop him from being an engineer.

As he kept talking I noticed a slight Spanish accent, which to me rather embellished the language of Debs and Whitman.

"Are you Spanish?"

"No, I am a Puerto Rican." The answer flashed back with a voice full of pride and dignity that was exhilarating, coming from so young a person. Then he added

"I was brought up here when I was eight. I am now almost fifteen."

"I am a Puerto Rican too," I said.

And from there on we continued our conversation in Spanish.

He told me about the crowded conditions in which he lives. Three brothers and a sister, living in one room on a top floor, back. No father. Only a mother needle-trade worker, who has to work long hours overtime to feed the family.

[1]Published in *The Worker* (February 7, 1960): 10.

I noticed that all the books the boy was carrying from the library were on elementary science. There was one on inventions.

"Where do you do your reading?" I asked, as I thought of that one-room "apartment" where cooking, washing, eating and sleeping had to be done almost simultaneously by six human beings.

"I do my reading on the roof," he replied. During the winter I read in the wooden shack leading to the roof. (Shades of Abraham Lincoln!) During the summer I just open the door to the roof and sit on an old milk box with my back to the roof entrance and just READ.

The boy gave such emphasis to the word READ as if he meant to say, "I read, read, read, and then read some more."

"In order to be an engineer," I said, "you must study a lot of mathematics, I mean arithmetic, algebra ... "

At the mention of algebra, the lad became excited. He got up and started talking a mile a minute, half in English and half in Spanish, and gesticulating as if reacting to a heated argument that he must have had with somebody.

"That's it, algebra, algebra, algebra! Yes algebra!" he shouted at me. "And they don't want to let me in on that algebra class! The only algebra class in the school!"

"And they don't let Emilio, my friend, get into that class either." The boy explained that Emilio also wanted to study engineering.

"Who doesn't let you into this algebra class?"

"The teacher, the principal. Yeah, I know I need a lot of math to be an engineer, but they don't let me in, they don't let me in, they don't let me in ... !"

"Are there any Puerto Ricans in this algebra class?"

"No, not one."

"Are you sure?"

"Of course, I'm sure! I know all the Puerto Ricans in the school."

"Are there no Negroes in that algebra class either?"

"No, no Negroes either." He answered this one with a surprised look, as if wondering whether I had a crystal ball.

Then he repeated slowly, looking deep into my eyes as something was dawning in his mind: "No, no Negroes either in that algebra class."

The Negro in Puerto Rican History[1]

Readers have asked me many times about the Negro in Puerto Rico. Also quite a number of persons attending classes and talks that I have been privileged to deliver at small gatherings have been interested in the Negro in our Puerto Rican nation.

No better occasion than Negro History Week to present this question at least in its most general historical background.

Many years before the discovery of America, the Portuguese were dealing in the slave trade between the western shores of Africa and Spain and Portugal. As a result, many authorities claim, cities like Lisbon and Seville had large districts populated by freed and enslaved Negroes and mulattoes. The government had to assign Negro judges and other municipal personnel in these cities in order to better conduct city affairs.

Juan Latino, professor of the University of Granada, one of the most famous universities of the medieval period, was a Negro.[2]

Puerto Rico

So when the Spaniards came to Puerto Rico in the first years of the sixteenth century, they brought with them Negroes born or reared in Spain as domestic and house servants.

As a result of the massacre of Indians in rebellions against the Spaniards, and the hard work from sunrise to sunset, many thousands of Indians were exterminated while others took refuge in the mountains or rowed away to other islands of the Caribbean.

The scarcity of Indian manpower required primarily to get the precious gold for the Spaniards and to attend to the primitive agricultural needs of

---

[1]Published in *The Worker* (February 7, 1960).
[2]See Arturo Shomburg's article "Juan Latino," *African Times and Orient Review* 1 (1913): 223–24.

the Spaniards for food forced the Spanish settlers to look toward Africa as the source for mass importation of slaves into Puerto Rico.

There was a priest, Bartolomé de las Casas who, in his idealistic concern for the Indians, helped influence the decision, already forced by economic necessity, to import African slaves. His lived to regret his recommendation.

There are indications throughout this initial period of Puerto Rican history that the first Negroes brought from Europe as house servants helped the native Indians in many of their rebellions and their flight into the hinterland.

Abolitionists

The most prominent Puerto Rican abolitionists were Dr. Ramón Emeterio Betances, a graduate of the University of Paris; Segundo Ruiz Belvis, a talented lawyer and patriot; and Julio L. Vizcarrondo, a journalist.[3]

According to a decree passed by General Pezuela, Spanish governor of Puerto Rico, the price for the freedom of a baby born in slavery was $25. Dr. Betances used to come to the door of the church on Sunday and, as the baby slaves were bought out from their christening ceremonies, he paid the $25 price. Thus many Negro men and women won freedom because of Dr. Betances, who was also the first to project the idea of independence for Puerto Rico.

Segundo Ruiz Belvis freed all the slaves that he had inherited. He went on a patriotic pilgrimage at the same time.

Branding

Among the barbarities practiced against the Negro slaves was branding with red hot irons to establish their identity as the property of certain masters. The practice of branding was called "El Carimbo." In 1784, "El Carimbo" was abolished by law in Puerto Rico.

By the beginning of the nineteenth century, many of the nations of the world started to set dates for prohibiting the importation of slaves from Africa, if not to end slavery itself. Contraband in slaves increased, however, as the result of this prohibition.

When the development of the "hacienda" system, based on slavery, ceased to be profitable, the agitation of the abolitionists increased. There were a number of instances of rebellion among the slaves.

[3]Julio L. Vizcarrondo (1830–1889) freed his own slaves in 1854 as a symbol of his abolitionist ideals. Slavery was finally abolished in Puerto Rico in 1883.

On March 22, 1873, the Spanish parliament in Madrid, forced by the outbursts of rebellion amoung the slaves and anti-slavery public sentiment, finally abolished slavery in Puerto Rico.

About 29,000 slaves were set free and every slave-owner was compensated by the government.

"But how about the position of the Negro in Puerto Rico today?" you ask.

That's right. You see, I like to start at the beginning. Suppose I tell you all about that next week.

The Negro in Puerto Rico Today[1]

In my column during Negro History Week I gave a historical background of the Negro in Puerto Rico. I promised a second column in which I would deal with this question from the standpoint of the position of the Negro and Negro-white relationships in Puerto Rico today. This is it.

Let me say from the start that the question of the Negro today in Puerto Rico would require a series of columns.

The bibliography on the Negro today in Puerto Rico is very poor. The best known works are Dr. C. Rosario's book, "El Negro," and Dr. Tomás Blanco's lecture on this subject delivered in Havana, Cuba, some years ago. These two examples of studies in this field are, however, poor and vacillating.[2] Dr. Tomás Blanco's *Prontuario Histórico* is perhaps the best short analysis of Puerto Rican history available, but his lecture on the Negro is inadequate.

On the other hand, on slavery in Puerto Rico, or on the life of the Negro in previous centuries, there is a well documented history and abundant material in Coll y, Toste, Brau, Tapia, and other Puerto Rican historians, poets and writers ... enough to fill a good many volumes.[3]

But as to the Negro in Puerto Rican life TODAY ... that's another matter.

It seems that for those trained to give us such studies, as well as for those writers who could throw light on this question on the basis of their experiences and their sensitivity to the whole thing, it is a very "delicate" question, to say the least. This attitude, of course, reflects on the very nature and composition of Puerto Rican society today.

[1]Published in *The Worker* (March 13, 1960): 10.

[2]Tomás Blanco (1900–1975), intellectual leader of the Generation of 1930, is author of the essay *El prejuicio racial en Puerto Rico* (1942).

[3]Cayetano Coll y Toste (1850–1930) compiled the 13 volumes that constitute the *Boletín histórico de Puerto Rico* (1914–1927). Salvador Brau (1842–1912) was appointed official historian of Puerto Rico in 1903 until his death. Alejandro Tapia y Rivera (1826–1882) compiled the series of historical documents known as *Biblioteca histórica de Puerto Rico*.

The fact that we in Puerto Rico have been "miscegenating" for the last four hundred years and more has created a series of illusions, if not downright hypocritical attitudes, that have been passed down as truth for many years.

One such illusion is that there is no such thing as race prejudice in Puerto Rico, that we are ALL Puerto Ricans, and that is all. No difference.

To believe this is to ignore the very origin of the white Puerto Ricans' and the Negro Puerto Ricans' ancestors, how they came to Puerto Rico, and the obligatory relationship of master and slave that was established right from the beginning. To believe this illusion is to ignore the tremendous pressure exerted by those in power under Spanish domination to make sure that all the lies of a "superior" and "inferior" race be perpetuated in life and in mind in order to justify their inhuman exploitation of slaves.

Then came American imperialism, using racism and discrimination to justify the exploitation of the Negro right here in the U.S.A. and of the other colonial and semi-colonial people all over the world. The U. S. representatives of the American imperialist "way of life" and its Puerto Rican stooges accelerated and perfected this process of catering to the racist ideas of the imperialist power.

Today, racial prejudice, racial discrimination and the barring of opportunities is practiced not crudely or openly. It is done suavely. With finesse. WE are "civilized," you know.

Today the imperialist "superior" race concept of the South permeates almost all of Washington and Wall Street, and dominates their policies. The bosses just insinuate. And the stooges do the dirty work.

Today, because growing racism in Puerto Rico is subtle, the aspiring young Negro is not branded with "El Carimbo" on his body. But he is branded in his soul, in his character, in his personality with "El Carimbo" of hypocrisy, of double talk, of shallow, meaningless and useless sentimentality and poetry.

In July, 1950, Ciro Alegría, the Peruvian novelist and author of *Broad and Alien is the World*, was living in Puerto Rico with a talk to the evening students of the High School of Santurce and articles in *El Mundo*. When he touched on this subject, which everybody tries to avoid discussing thoroughly and frankly, he created an uproar.

On February 9 this year in the Puerto Rican Legislature, bill No. 348 was forced out of committee by Independence representative José Feliu Pesquera. According to the editorial in *El Mundo* of February 1, this bill was "placidly sleeping in the protective bosom of a committee for the last two years."

Bill 348 provides that "it shall be illegal to deny the selling or leasing of any dwelling because of race, creed, color or political belief."

The very fact that the need was felt to pass such a law proves that there is discrimination and race prejudice in Puerto Rico.

After much parliamentary maneuvering, the bill was sent back to the Committee.

This happened on February 9, 1960, of the year of our ... Luis Muñoz Marín.

Puerto Rican Migrant Labor[1]

There are two ways of reaching New York from Puerto Rico: one is by flying directly from Puerto Rico; the other is by car or bus after you have left Puerto Rico for other cities in the U. S.

An increasing number of Puerto Ricans are coming through the Holland Tunnel after being picked up along the highway by a sympathetic driver. There are others, not so fortunate, who by hiking day and night finally cross the George Washington Bridge and enter the city. They come not from Chicago or Philadelphia but from one of those concentration camps in which the Puerto Rican seasonal workers are kept, for all intents and purposes, in practical slavery, under the worst living conditions possible, getting beatings and very little pay when the "deductions" are made against the pennies per hour they receive as wages.

This was the problem that a congressional subcommittee of the Education and Labor Committee, under the chairmanship of Adam Clayton Powell, was investigating at an open hearing at the Federal Court Building with Rep. Herbert Zelenko (D-NY) heading the subcommittee. The other two members on this subcommittee were Rep. Dominick Daniels (D-NY) and Rep. David Martin (R-Neb). The declarations of the Puerto Rican migrant worker, Fermín López Rosado, were undoubtedly the most dramatic and significant made during the hearings.

López Rosado has a wife and five children living in Puerto Rico. When he handed over the pay envelopes for the subcommittee investigators to add up all the "deductions" made by the farm association for which he was working in New Jersey, it was revealed that he was getting $5.43 for 40 hours of work. Yes, $5.43 for FORTY HOURS! Another envelope showed that he received $5.53 for 52 hours of work "after deductions" for social security, health insurance, and part payment for his flight ticket from Puerto Rico.

[1]Published in *The Worker* (June 6, 1961).

López Rosado further testified that on May 14 one of the guards of the "Glassboro Service Association" beat him so badly that he had to go to the hospital for injuries in the head, back and legs.

When he protested, he was given five minutes to pack up his belongings and leave the camp.

There are around 15,000 Puerto Rican migrant workers in other camps in Pennsylvania, Connecticut, upstate New York and as far down as Virginia and Florida.

Thirty-two Puerto Rican migrant workers, signed up to work on some farms in Long Island, were transported to Virginia without their knowledge or consent. There they were forced to work under worse conditions and lower wages.

Another glaring abuse reported by López Rosado was the common practice of fixing the scale on which the tomato, asparagus and other vegetable baskets were weighed when the laborer brought in the quantity he had gathered during a certain period. Usually the company cheats the migrant worker of 30% of the weight of the produce he has picked in the fields.

As López Rosado recounted his experience and the numerous ways that he was being exploited, tears rolled down his cheeks because, with all those long hours of work in the fields, he hardly had any money to send to his wife and five children in Puerto Rico.

Fifteen thousand Puerto Rican migrant workers, plus other thousands from Jamaica and the other West Indies. Plus thousands from Mexico ... and the white and Negro exploited workers from our own South.

This is a problem to which we progressives should be giving more thought—and action.

Arthur Schomburg and Negro History[1]

Nothing is more appropriate for Negro History Week than to write a few lines about Arturo Schomburg, a Puerto Rican Negro born in San Juan, Puerto Rico in 1874. (It gives me special pleasure to write about him as I had the privilege of knowing him back in the thirties.)

Today the Schomburg Collection, considered the greatest compilation in the world of books, manuscripts, pictures, prints and works of art on the Negro, stands at 103 W. 135 St. in New York City as the result of the life-long effort of this great Puerto Rican Negro.

The story goes that on assigning homework, a Spanish teacher during Schomburg's boyhood in Puerto Rico said, pointing to various boys, "For tomorrow, you bring some facts about the history of the white race ... and you about the Indian race ... and you about the yellow race." Little Arturo Schomburg raised his hand and asked, "And how about the Negro race?" "The Negro has no history," was the curt answer of the Spanish teacher.

From then on Arturo Schomburg decided to dedicate his life to gathering everything he could about the Negro past.

If you read the minutes of some of the Puerto Rican clubs existing in the early [eighteen] nineties in New York City, you will find the name of Arturo Schomburg as an active member. He was the secretary of "Las Dos Antillas," a club of Puerto Ricans and Cubans in New York City actively working for the independence of Cuba and Puerto Rico from Spanish oppression.

Arthur Schomburg went all over the world searching for books, paintings, manuscripts and all kinds of data on the Negro past. Schomburg started by gathering material on great Puerto Rican Negroes like José Campeche Jordán (1752–1809), considered Puerto Rico's greatest painter, whose works were successfully exhibited in Rome. In arguing with his young Puerto Rican white friends, Schomburg liked to point out the work of Rafael Cordero, a cigarmaker and teacher who taught many of Puerto Rico's greatest names in literature and politics how to read and write.

[1]Published in *The Worker* (February 11, 1962): 9.

98

Arthur Schomburg discovered that Juan Pareja, one of Spain's great painters, had been a Negro slave of Diego Velázquez, the famous Spanish painter. Velázquez taught Juan Pareja how to paint. Schomburg traced one of Pareja's paintings all the way from Europe to a store-room in New York City where the painting had remained unrecognized for years.[2]

J. A. Rogers, writing on Arthur Schomburg and his life's works collection, says, "The field of information covered is vast and varied. There are subjects such as Zulu nursery rhymes printed in the Bantu language, books on anthropology, folklore, sociology, customs of the Negro in the Congo, Guinea, Ashanti, the West Indies and the wilds of South America; sermons on slavery by ex-slaves; travel, poetry, drama, and culture in general."

Rogers also writes that in 1926 the Carnegie Corporation of New York City paid Schomburg 10,000 dollars for his collection, "which was about a fifth of its intrinsic value."[3]

There are no fewer than five thousand books and a few thousand pamphlets in many languages aside from the many interesting and beautiful works of art done by Negroes or by whites about the Negro at this most outstanding collection, right here in the heart of your city.

Why not make it a point to visit the Schomburg Collection this week— Negro History Week?

[2]See Shomburg's article, "In Quest of Juan Pareja," *Crisis* 34 (1927): 153–54, 174.

[3]J. H. Clarke, ed., "Arthur Schomburg, the Sherlock Holmes of Negro History," *World Great Men of Color* (New York: Macmillan, 1972): 449–52.

Statement by Jesús Colón to the
Walter Committee on Un-American Activities[1]

It is clear to all who have followed the antics of the so-called Committee on Un-American Activities that it has served to protect and mask the real Un-American activities of the Ku Klux Klan and The White Citizens Council. This committee has not cared to investigate the activities of these proven un-American groups, while it keeps continuously investigating and persecuting groups and individuals who have dedicated long years of their lives in the defense of all that is free, true, and in the best traditions of democracy in the United States.

Instead of this committee harassing the Puerto Rican people here in New York and unlawfully invading Puerto Rico, it is high time that the people in the United States start recognizing this committee for what it is—an instrument of U. S. reaction to thwart, misrepresent, and destroy all attempts by the democratic-loving persons of this country to keep and strengthen their constitution, fought for by the founders of the United States and defended and further enriched by the Lincolns and Franklin Roosevelts that followed them.

By this inquisitorial invasion of Puerto Rico, U. S. reactionary and imperialist forces acting through the so-called Un-American Committee are adding a new venture to their already disgraceful record against freedom and democracy in this country. This committee is invading the Commonwealth of Puerto Rico without a mandate or even an ordinary invitation from that country.

We might well ask ourselves: What is the next Latin American country to be invaded by this committee: Panama, Costa Rica, Guatemala?

[1]Statement read at Foley Square Courthouse, New York City, November 16, 1959. Colón also recounts this experience in *As I See It From Here* in the columns "I Appear Before the Un-Americans," *The Worker* (November, 29, 1959), and "The Un-Americans and the Americans," *The Worker* (December 6, 1959).

100

The Puerto Rican nation was forcibly invaded by the military might of American imperialism in 1898. The Puerto Ricans, fooled at that time by the never fulfilled promises of General Miles, are being forcibly invaded again by this witch hunt committee to question and harass two hundred workers, intellectuals, and freedom-loving Puerto Rican patriots to see if they can do by fear, intimidation, and jailings, what American imperialism has been unable to do by starvation, military, naval and atomic occupation, one crop agricultural economy, sweat shop industrialization with barely living wages, and the destruction of the social, historical, and cultural traditions of a people.

It is clear that this committee is being used as an attack against Fidel Castro and the Cuban people's revolutionary and anti-imperialist movement—a revolutionary movement supported by all the freedom-loving groups and parties in Cuba, including the Popular Socialist Party.

Fidel Castro and the Cuban people have dared to defy American imperialism by refusing to compromise with Wall Street and Washington and going all out for far overdue basic changes and agrarian reforms in Cuba's economic life and social and cultural structure. This has brought new hope and confidence to the anti-imperialist struggle in all the countries of Latin America.

It is in the best tradition of democracy in this country to support the Cuban people and Fidel Castro these days.

The Cuban Revolution with Fidel Castro at its helm has been slandered and misrepresented in the United States, while the proven enemies and aggressors of Cuba and its revolution here have been pampered, televised, and officially interviewed by Congressional Committees in Washington.

Puerto Rico is being used now as a naval, military, aerial, and atomic base by American imperialism in seeing to it that the other Latin American nations do not follow the Cuban example.

There are millions of Latin Americans living in the United States. Cubans, Mexicans, Puerto Ricans, and many thousands from the other republics living here, who support in the main the progressive leaders and movements in this country. As in New York City with the Puerto Ricans—followers of the late Vito Marcantonio—the Spanish-speaking people here are becoming a deciding force politically and otherwise.

The invasion of the Walter Un-American Activities Committee into Puerto Rico, the subpoenas and inquisitions which about two hundred in Puerto Rico will have to go through, not only show the arrogant and imperialist methods of Wall Street and Washington in violating Congressional laws and agreements with the Commonwealth of Puerto Rico, but also show the need for complete and absolute independence for Puerto Rico. This would be the only way that Puerto Rico would be able to bar, through the international body of laws respected by all sovereign nations, the shameful invasion of individual and national rights of Puerto Ricans by such phony and unconstitutional outfits as this so-called Un-American Committee.

I will never cooperate with this Un-American Committee in its aim to destroy the Bill of Rights and the other constitutional rights of the people.

Certainly I will never cooperate with the efforts of this committee to take away the few liberties the Puerto Ricans have today nor to set a barrier to the only solution for Puerto Rico and the Puerto Ricans: complete and absolute independence.

> ¡POR LA INDEPENDENCIA DE PUERTO RICO!
> ¡POR EL FINAL TRIUNFO DEL SOCIALISMO EN PUER-
> TO RICO!
> ¡POR LA REVOLUCION CUBANA Y SU PROGRAMA
> REVOLUCIONARIO ANTI-IMPERIALISTA!
> ¡POR LA ELIMINACIÓN DEL UN-AMERICAN ACTIV-
> ITIES COMMITTEE QUE ES UN DESPRESTIGIO PARA LA
> VERDADERA DEMOCRACIA EN ESTADOS UNIDOS!
> ¡ABAJO EL IMPERIALISMO YANQUI EN LA AMER-
> ICA LATINA!

Biographical Chronology

1901   Born January 20 in Cayey, Puerto Rico.
1917   Becomes Editor of *Adelante*, newspaper of the Central Grammar School in San Juan, Puerto Rico.
       Arrives in New York as a stowaway on the ship S.S. Carolina. Settles in Brooklyn, New York.
1918   Founding member of the first Puerto Rican Committee of the Socialist Party in New York.
1923   Founding member and first Secretary General of the organization Alianza Obrera Puertorriqueña in New York.
1922   Graduates from Boys High Evening School in Brooklyn.
1923–1924   Becomes a regular overseas contributor to *Justicia*, newspaper of the Federación Libre de Trabajadores in Puerto Rico.
1925   Marries Rufa Concepción (Concha) Fernández.
1926   Founding member of the Ateneo Obrero Hispano.
1927–1928   Becomes a regular contributor to the newspaper *Gráfico*.
1928   Founding member of the Liga Puertorriqueña e Hispana and editor of its bulletin.
1933   Joins the Communist Party.
1934   Founding member of Mutualista Obrera Puertor-riqueña.
1943–1944   Publishes his column *Lo que el pueblo me dice* in the newspaper *Pueblos Hispanos*.
1944   Becomes official organizer of the Hispanic Section of the International Workers' Order, a multinational fraternal organization.

1946–1947 Becomes a regular contributor to the Spanish newspaper *Liberación*.
194? President, Sociedad Fraternal Cervantes.
1953? Runs for the New York State Assembly on the American Labor Party ticket.
1955? Runs for the New York State Senate on the American Labor Party ticket.
1955–1957 Publishes his weekly column *As I See It From Here* in *The Daily Worker*.
1957–1961 Becomes a contributing editor to the magazine *Mainstream*.
1958–1968 Continues his weekly column *As I See From Here* in *The Worker*.
1959 Is investigated by the House Un-American Activities Committee and in response writes a statement read at the Foley Square Courthouse.
1961 Publishes the first edition of *A Puerto Rican in New York and Other Sketches*.
Teaches at Jefferson School.
1968–1971 Publishes his column *Puerto Rican Notes* in *The Daily World*.
1969 Runs for New York City Controller on the Communist Party ticket.
1970 His second wife Clara Colón, a Jewish-American, dies after a prolonged bout with cancer.
1974 Dies in New York at the age of 73.
1984 A new edition of *A Puerto Rican in New York and Other Sketches* (New York: International Publishers) appears with a Foreword by Juan Flores.
1983 Colón's papers are donated to the Centro de Estudios Puertorriqueños Library at Hunter College.

Bibliography of Jesús Colón's Writings

I. Articles Published in *Gráfico*

Date	Title	Pseudonym Used
5/9/27	En neoyorkino	Miquis Tiquis
8/7/27	De la Universidad de la Vida	
10/9/27	En neoyorkino	Miquis Tiquis
10/23/27	En neoyorkino	Miquis Tiquis
10/30/27	En neoyorkino	Miquis Tiquis
11/6/27	En neoyorkino	Miquis Tiquis
12/4/27	En neoyorkino	Miquis Tiquis
12/25/27	En neoyorkino	Miquis Tiquis
1/8/28	En neoyorkino	Miquis Tiquis
3/4/28	En neoyorkino	Miquis Tiquis
6/29/28	"¿Quiénes son los judíos?"	
7/15/28	Mis vecinos	Miquis Tiquis
7/22/28	Nuestra gente	Miquis Tiquis
8/12/28	"¿Quiénes son los judíos?"	
8/5/28	Cartas inmorales a mi novia	Pericles Espada
8/19/28	Cartas inmorales a mi novia	Pericles Espada
9/9/28	Cartas inmorales a mi novia	Pericles Espada
10/7/28	Cartas inmorales a mi novia	Pericles Espada
10/28/28	Cartas inmorales a mi novia	Pericles Espada

II. Articles published in *Pueblos Hispanos*

Colón's Column: *Lo que el pueblo me dice*

2/27/43: 3, 4, 8	Salvemos a los refugiados españoles de Africa del Norte
2/6/43: 3–4	Basta de apaciguar a Franco
2/13/43: 3	¿Por qué lloras—, mujer?
3/20/43: 3, 9	Lo que el pueblo me dice
3/27/43: 3, 11	Jesús Colón éste es tu periódico
4/3/43: 3, 8, 12	Escribe esa carta
4/10/43: 3, 12	Lo que el pueblo me dice
4/17/43: 3	Los otros Estados Unidos
4/24/43: 3	Sociedades y sociedades
5/1/43: 3	Los judíos y nosotros
5/8/43: 3, 7	De todos los argumentos, el más pobre
5/15/43: 3	Argumento número dos: Somos muy pequeños para ser libres
5/22/43: 3, 5, 11	Ya tenemos un coro de voces puertorriqueñas
5/29/43: 3, 10	Luchadores del porvenir puertorriqueño de Brooklyn organizan un certamen de nuevo tipo
6/5/43: 3, 10	Yo vi una gran película
6/12/43: 3	Una palabra a los que están bien
6/19/43: 3, 10	John L. Lewis no es el héroe que quieren pintarnos
6/26/43: 3, 10	Cuidado, Harlem
7/3/43: 3, 10	Lo que el pueblo me dice
7/10/43: 3, 10	Mi barbero y mi amigo
7/17/43: 3, 7	Puerto Rico es también una nación
7/24/43: 3, 10	Hacia una gran institución puertorriqueña
7/31/43: 3, 5, 10	El mundo avanza
8/7/43: 3, 10	Acto de presencia de estudio y de acción
8/14/43: 3, 10	Hace falta una estatua
8/21/43: 3, 10	Las películas de guerra y las películas cómicas

III. Articles Published in *Liberación*

4/24/46: ?	Españoles, puertorriqueños e hispanoamericanos marcharán el 1 de mayo
5/24/46: 1, 5	Cuál debe ser nuestra posición ante el problema político de Puerto Rico
6/3/46: 3	Cómo defender la independencia de Puerto Rico en Nueva York
7/10/46: 1, 7	Cómo defender la independencia de Pto. Rico en Nueva York
7/17/46: 1, 7	Cómo defender la independencia de Pto. Rico en Nueva York
8/18/46: 1	Por qué No la Autonomía ... : Nuestra posición ante el status político de Puerto Rico
8/4/46: 1	Comedia de un gobernador para Pto. Rico: ¿Cuál debe ser nuestra posición ante el status político de Puerto Rico?

IV. Articles Published in *The Daily Worker*

From November 21, 1955, to October 8, 1957, Colón's column *As I See It From Here* appeared in *The Daily Worker*. The column would later continue to be published in *The Worker*.

Date	Title
11/21/55	Columbus Discovers Puerto Rico
11/28/55	What's in a Name
12/5/55	Puerto Rican Music
12/12/55	To the Greatest Man in the City of X
12/19/55	A Hero in the Junk Truck
1/2/56	Minimum Wage Struggle in Puerto Rico
1/9/56	The Struggle Continues
1/16/56	A Judge in New Jersey
1/23/56	How to Know The Puerto Rican
1/30/56	Is Language a Barrier

Date	Title
2/6/56	Trujillo's Fair of Blood
2/13/56	Casals in Puerto Rico
2/20/56	We Call Him Foster
2/27/56	Sarah
3/5/56	The Library Looks at the Puerto Ricans
3/12/56	Puerto Rican Music at Hunter College
3/19/56	Civil Rights in Puerto Rico
3/26/56	Pisagua
4/2/56	And Fuchik Looked as Confident
4/9/56	If Instead of a Professor
4/17/56	First May Day in Puerto Rico
4/24/56	What a Parade
5/1/56	Maceo
5/8/56	Rivera Back in Mexico
5/15/56	Wanted: A Statue
5/22/56	Invitation to the Theater
5/29/56	More on Topical Theater and "The Desperadoes"
6/5/56	Little Things in Spain
6/13/56	"Dr." Ramón Ruiz: Agent of the FBI
6/19/56	Something to Read
6/27/56	Little Things Are Big
7/4/56	For the Stay-at-Homes
7/10/56	Marcelino
8/7/56	What Shall I Write About
8/14/56	The Visitor
8/21/56	Two Books of Poetry
8/28/56	It Happened One Winter's Night
9/4/56	Hollywood Rewrites History
9/11/56	More on Santiago
9/18/56	Taking Over the Mall
9/25/56	Chinese Opera in Latin America
10/2/56	What D'Ya Read?
10/9/56	The Story of Ana Roque
10/16/56	Easy Job, Good Wages
10/23/56	An Appeal to Tradition
10/30/56	Voice through a Window

Date	Title
11/6/56	Me, Candido I
11/13/56	Hiawatha into Spanish
11/20/56	Red Roses for Me
11/27/56	My Private Hall of Fame
12/4/56	The Lady Who Lived Near the Statue of a Man on a Horse
12/11/56	Puerto Rican Briefs
12/18/56	Briefs from New York
12/25/56	Looking Just a Little Forward
1/1/57	Stowaway
1/8/57	Reading in the Bathtub
1/15/57	Name in Latin
1/22/57	Goodbye Goyita
1/29/57	"Jewish Life" Anthology, a Book To Be Remembered
2/5/57	On the Docks It Was Cold
1/12/57	I Heard a Man Crying
2/19/57	Greetings: Elias Lafertte
2/26/57	My First Strike
3/5/57	Rudyard Kipling and I
3/12/57	The Origin of Latin American Dances
3/19/57	2 Concerts at Town Hall
3/26/57	Hello Sam
4/2/57	She Actually Pinched Me!
4/9/57	Because He Spoke in Spanish
4/16/57	"I Made It!" "I Sold It!" "I Bought It!"
4/23/57	Grandma, Please Don't Come
4/30/57	The Day My Father Got Lost
5/7/57	Ed Murrow's TV Report on the Puerto Ricans
5/14/57	Pilgrimage of Prayer
5/21/57	I Went to School Friday—in Washington D.C.
5/28/57	A Raincoat and a Hat
6/4/57	Lucía and Her Soul
6/11/57	The Rosenbergs
6/18/57	Vacation Is a Problem
6/25/57	Children Too Need a Vacation
7/2/57	Phrase Heard in a Bus

Date	Title
7/9/57	Jeannie
7/16/57	Meetings I Have Been to
8/5/57	Fifth Anniversary
8/20/57	Puerto Rican Smith Act Repealed
8/27/57	The Unwritten Gag Law
9/3/57	Unwritten Gag Law (II)
9/10/57	To the Puerto Ricans of the Lower East Side
9/17/57	Before the Opening
9/24/57	El 'Cuco'
10/1/57	150,000
10/8/57	Little Rock
12/3/57	A Raincoat and a Hat
12/10/57	'Jewish Life' Anthology, a Book to be Treasured
12/17/57	Vacation is a Problem

V. Articles published in *Mainstream*

In February 1957, Jesus Colón became a contributing editor to the monthly magazine *Mainstream*. The majority of his writings published in *Mainstream* were later included in *A Puerto Rican in New York and Other Sketches* (New York: Masses and Mainstream, 1961).

2/57: 7–19	Lucia and Her Soul
	The Visitor
	Easy Job, Good Wages
	The Mother, the Younger Daughter, Myself, and All of Us
	It Happened One Winter's Night
	Little Things Are Big
4/58: 30–32	I Heard a Man Crying
6/59: 56–59	Book Reviews of *Island in the City* by Dan Wakefield; *Up from Puerto Rico* by Elena Padilla; and *The Puerto Ricans* by Christopher Rand
9/60: 42	Kipling and I
5/61: 70	José Martí Today

VI. Articles Published in *The Worker*

From January 1958 through September 1961, *The Worker* was published weekly. In October 1961, the newspaper expanded to include an additional midweek edition. The last page of this edition was called *El Trabajador*, directed at the Spanish-speaking population of New York. *The Worker* was last published in New York on July 14, 1968 and then became *The Daily World*.

Colón's Column: *As I See It From Here*

Date	Title
1/5/58	The Three Parades
1/12/58	Those Who Talk to Themselves
1/18/58	Two Parades
2/9/58	Martí, Freedom Fighter
2/23/58	Is This the End?
3/2/58	Marching in the Snow
3/9/58	Latin-American Manifesto
3/16/58	The Canary
3/23/58	The Galíndez Case
3/23/58	A Growing Minority
4/6/58	Colonial Showplace
4/13/58	Coalition in Colombia
4/20/58	Colombia's Communists
4/27/58	May Day Abroad
5/4/58	Death of a Hero
5/18/58	Nixon's Trip
5/25/58	Why Nixon Went to Bolivia
6/1/58	Spain's 14th of April
6/8/58	Memorial Days
6/15/58	Juan Ramón Jiménez
6/22/58	Moving Time
6/29/58	As I See It from Here
8/3/58	Crisis in Venezuela

Date	Title
8/10/58	Elections in Chile
8/17/58	More about Chile
8/24/58	The Argentine Way
8/31/58	A Get Together vs. Trujillo
9/7/58	As I See It From Here
9/14/58	The Powell Campaign
9/21/58	The Rockefeller Campaign
9/28/58	Rockefeller and the Roosevelt Tradition
10/5/58	The Question of Voting for Your "Own Kind"
10/12/58	As I See It From Here
10/19/58	As I See It From Here
10/26/58	Bronx Puerto Ricans and the Democrats
11/2/58	A Book about Puerto Ricans
11/9/58	A Visitor Reports on the Soviet Union
11/16/58	Ten to 30 Years for 2 Cigarettes
11/23/58	Puerto Ricans Continue to Vote Democrat
11/30/58	Queens and More Queens
12/7/58	As I See It From Here
12/14/58	As I See It From Here
12/21/58	As I See It From Here
1/4/59	As I See It From Here
1/11/59	The End of Batista's Regime, and The New Beginning for Cuba
1/18/59	As I See It From Here
1/25/59	As I See It From Here
2/8/59	As I See It From Here
2/15/59	As I See It From Here
2/22/59	As I See It From Here
3/1/59	As I See It From Here
3/8/59	As I See It From Here
3/22/59	As I See It From Here
3/29/59	As I See It From Here
4/5/59	Chile's Communists
4/12/59	As I See It From Here
4/19/59	As I See It From Here
4/26/59	As I See It From Here

Date	Title
5/3/59	May Days
5/10/59	Waiting for Castro
5/24/59	The Plot Against Cuba
5/31/59	Panama
6/7/59	Panama (Conclusion)
6/28/59	The Beginning of the End for Trujillo
7/5/59	Racism in Glendale and Ridgewood
7/12/59	As I See It From Here
7/19/59	As I See It From Here
7/26/59	As I See It From Here
8/2/59: 10	As I See It From Here
8/9/59: 10	As I See It From Here
8/16/59: 10	As I See It From Here
8/23/59: 10	As I See It From Here
8/30/59: 10	As I See It From Here
9/6/59: 10	As I See It From Here
9/13/59: 10	As I See It From Here
9/20/59: 10	As I See It From Here
9/27/59: 6	As I See It From Here
10/4/59: 10	As I See It From Here
10/11/59: 9	The Meaning of Algebra
11/8/59: 10	Spotlight on Latin America
11/15/59: 10	A Friend Becomes a Comrade
11/22/59: 10	From the Puerto Rican Communists
11/29/59: 10	I Appear before the UnAmericans
12/6/59: 10	The UnAmericans and the Americans
12/13/59: 10	THANKS!
12/20/59: 10	"Pan Americanism and Latin Americanism"
12/27/59: 10	Mikoyan in Mexico
1/3/60: 10	Latin-American Women's Congress
1/10/60: 10	Latin-American Women's Congress—Part 2
1/17/60: 10	Latin American Youth Congress
1/24/60: 10	1,323
1/31/60: 10	What the Women Said
2/7/60: 10	The Negro in Puerto Rican History
2/21/60: 10	A Poem to Visit with

Date	Title
2/28/60: 10	Soviet Exhibition in Havana
3/6/60: 10	Ike's First Stop
3/13/60: 10	The Negro in Puerto Rico Today
3/20/60: 10	Argentina Will Vote Blank
3/27/60: 10	Ike in Latin America
4/3/60: 7	Ike's Boner
4/10/60: 7	Latin American Highlights
4/17/60: 7	On Being Honored
4/24/60: 7	Spotlight on Latin America
5/1/60: 8	Puerto Rico's First May Day
5/8/60: 4	The Double Life of Muñoz Marín
5/15/60: 4	What is Happening in Venezuela
5/22/60: 4	Spotlight on Latin America
5/29/60: 4	"Patria o Muerte" Is Cuba's Slogan
6/5/60: 4	Questions and Answers
6/12/60: 4	Those Who Help the Chilean People
6/19/60: 4	For the Vacation Stay-at-Homes
7/17/60: 4	Oil, Sugar and Cuba
7/24/60: 4	How Stupid Can the State Department Get?
7/31/60: 4	Naciones sin "Income Tax"
8/7/60: 4	¿Es El Partido Comunista un Agente de Rusia?
8/14/60: 4	Sierra Maestra
8/21/60: 4	Youth Congress
8/28/60: 4	Briefs from and about Cuba
9/4/60: 4	Estoy en Cuba
9/11/60: 4	Cuba sí, Yankees no!
9/18/60: 4	Cuba is Like This
9/25/60: 4	The Golden Calf
10/9/60: 4	Harlem in Havana
10/16/60: 4	¿Por quién votar en noviembre?
10/23/60: 4	¿Por quién votar en noviembre?
10/30/60: 4	Cuban Briefs
11/6/60: 4	Ricardo the Indestructible
11/13/60: 4	Latin American Protests Threats against Cuba
11/27/60: 4	Independence for Puerto Rico
12/4/60: 4	Khruschev y Puerto Rico

Date	Title
12/11/60: 4	"Accidents" in Trujillo's Land
12/18/60: 4	Conversation in a Waiting Room
12/25/60: 4	A Puerto Rican Cultural Center
1/1/61: 4	The Situation in Venezuela
1/8/61: 4	Two Poems by Neruda
1/15/61: 4	Things Are Happening in Argentina
1/22/61: 4	Zero Hour for Cuba
1/29/61: 4	Marxists Discuss Negro Outlook
2/5/61: 4	Neruda's Poems Translated
2/12/61: 6	Light from the Santa María
2/19/61: 4	The First Time I Heard Foster
2/26/61: 4	Foster cumple ochenta años
3/5/61: 4	Elections in Argentina
3/19/61: 4	The Coconut in Your Kitchen
3/26/61: 4	Chile Goes to the Left
4/2/61: 8	The Peace Movement in Latin America
4/9/61: 8	The Trial of Francisco Molina
4/16/61: 8	Latin American Notes
4/23/61: 8	A New Era of Liberation for Latin America
4/30/61: 8	La farsa y la vergüenza de la invasión de Cuba
5/7/61: 6	Origen del desastre
5/14/61: 8	Ever Heard of Vieques?
5/21/61: 8	Un poema para hoy
5/28/61: 8	They Are Still Ahead of Us
6/4/61: 8	Puerto Rican Migrant Labor
6/11/61: 8	Are The Puerto Ricans for Castro?
6/18/61: 8	Latin American Briefs
6/25/61: 8	The Supreme Court Decision in Latin America
7/2/61: 9	It Was a Nice Party
7/9/61: 9	Trujillism without Trujillo
7/16/61: 9	Trickery or Tractors
7/30/61: 9	The Dominican Demonstration
8/20/61: 8	Cuban Writers' and Artists' Congress
8/27/61: 8	"Che" Guevara at Punta del Este
9/3/61: 8	El Día del Trabajo
9/10/61: 5	Pedro Albizu Campos' 70th Birthday Spurs

Date	Title
	Struggle for Freedom
9/17/61: 9	After the Parade
9/24/61: 8	Situación política y los puertorriqueños
10/1/61: 8	Catholics in Cuba
10/8/61: 8	The Puerto Ricans and Relief
10/15/61: 4	Balaguer Comes to the UN
10/17/61: 7	Puerto Rican Mother of 8 Evicted in Brooklyn
10/22/61: 9	Letters to Fidel
10/29/61: 9	A Poem to Don Pedro Albizu Campos
11/5/61: 4	Unity and Action in Dominican Republic
11/19/61: 8	Muddle in the Middle
11/26/61: 8	Melena del Sur, Cuba
12/3/61: 9	Poem of the 7th of November
12/10/61: 9	Destruyen derechos en nombre "La Ley"
12/24/61: 4	Who is Breaking Relations with Cuba?
1/7/62: 8	Facts of Kennedy Trip
1/14/62: 9	A New Poem By Neruda
1/21/62: 8	No More McCarran Law in Peru
1/28/62: 8	As Latin America Sees the McCarran Law
2/4/62: 7	Latin American Masses Mobilize for Cuba
2/11/62: 9	Arthur Schomburg and Negro History
2/18/62: 4	Chile CP is 40 Years Old
2/25/62: 9	Socialist Cuba
3/4/62: 9	The Hands of a Strikebreaker
3/11/62: 9	Fidel Castro's 'Disappearance'
4/1/62: 9	The Exploitation of Man by Man
4/8/62: 9	Explanations
4/15/62: 3	Havana Trial Bares Sordid Invasion Aims
4/29/62: 8	A Poem by Puerto Rico's Greatest Poet
5/6/62: 10	Confessions of an Invader
5/8/62: 4	Two Spanish Papers—And Just One Owner
5/20/62: 10	More San Román Letters
5/27/62: 11	Last of the San Román Letters
6/3/62: 10	A History of Cuba
6/10/62: 6	Background to the Strikes in Spain
6/17/62: 11	Spain Today

Date	Title
6/24/62: 11	Background in Venezuela
7/1/62: 11	Venezuela Today
7/15/62: 5	Guest Column
7/29/62: 7	Haya de la Torre's Perspective
8/5/62: 8	The Language of Puerto Rico
8/12/62: 8	Zig-Zag Language Policy in Puerto Rico
9/2/62: 10	Plebiscite for Puerto Rico?
9/30/62: 5	14 Bases Training Invaders of Cuba
10/7/62: 5	September 23, 1868
10/14/62: 8	Guerrillas in Venezuela
10/21/62: 8	Story of a Real Man
10/28/62: 8	Anti-Democratic Front in Chile
11/4/62: 5	Puerto Ricans and the Election
11/11/62: 5	Letter to Caroline
11/18/62: 5	Puerto Ricans Elected
11/25/62: 5	What Did Castro Say?
12/2/62: 5	Colombia's Crisis
12/9/62: 8	The Coming Dominican Elections
12/23/62: 8	The Front Window of the Subway Train
12/30/62: 8	And a Very Happy New Year
1/6/63: 8	From Words to Deeds
1/13/63: 8	The Prisoner Nobody Quotes
1/20/63: 8	Peru
1/27/63: 5	A Young Man Whistling
2/3/63: 5	Congress of Solidarity
2/10/63: 5	Framed Cubans
2/17/63: 5	Again Cuba: Why?
2/24/63: 8	InterAmerican Junta
3/5/63: 6	A Phrase that Won't Die
3/17/63: 5	Cuba's New Kind of Schooling
3/24/63: 8	Schools of Marxism-Leninism
4/2/63: 6	The Lady with the Family Tree
4/7/63: 8	Women's Day in Cuba
4/14/63: 9	The Battle of Playa Girón
4/23/63: 4	Chile's Municipal Elections
5/5/63: 8	Manuel Castro's Invention

Date	Title
5/19/63: 9	Voters' Rights
5/28/63: 7	Cuba Looks at Birmingham
6/9/63: 8	Raúl Rodríguez
7/2/63: 7	"I Give Castro Six Months"
7/16/63: 3	The Puerto Rican Parade
7/23/63: 4	U. S. Invasion of Puerto Rico is 65 Years Old
8/6/63: 4	Neo-Nazi Congress in Latin America
8/20/63: 4	The Puerto Ricans Will Be There
10/8/63: 2	Venezuelan Legislators Jailed; Immunity Violated
11/19/63: 4	Candidates and Issues in Venezuela's Election
11/19/63: 8	200 Delegates Fight for Fair Housing
12/3/63: 4	Mourners for Two Puerto Ricans Demand Probe of Patrol Cops
1/14/64: 2	Preparations Going Forward for One-Day School Boycott
2/16/64: 11	Negro, Puerto Rican Rally Builds Unity
8/11/64: 5	Pablo Neruda is 60 Years Old
8/23/64: 2	Muñoz Marín Bars 5th Term
8/30/64: 4	Dr. Allende Maps a More Democratic Chile
9/15/64: 4	García Lorca's Plays Get Wide Airing in Original Spanish
12/22/64: 7	Latin America Parley Maps Anti-Trust Stand
1/12/65: 6	New Head in Puerto Rico is Longtime Aide of Muñoz
7/20/65: 4	How Pentagon Invades Latin American Colleges
7/27/65: 8	Puerto Rican Candidates
10/10/65: 11	100 Puerto Rican Women Protest on Vietnam War
2/1/66: 4	Rightist Generals Refuse to Leave Domingo
2/8/66: 4	Lindsay Rebuffs Group of Puerto Ricans
3/1/66: 4	Colombia CP Stresses Front Against U. S. Imperialism
4/3/66: 12	Latin Americans March in NY Peace Parade
4/4/67: 7	Why Puerto Ricans Oppose the Coming Plebiscite
7/18/67: 6	Why the U. S. is Rushing Puerto Rican Plebiscites
11/21/67: 8	URSS celebra 50 años futuro glorioso de la humanidad

Date   Title

2/27/68   La otra Julia de Burgos
3/26/68   B'klyn Puerto Rican

The following article about Jesús Colón was published in *The Worker*.
1/20/63: 7   Book Review of *A Puerto Rican in New York*

VII. Articles Published in *The Daily World*

Colón's Column *Puerto Rican Notes* and Other Articles
Date   Title

7/20/68: 6   International Commentary
7/27/68: 6   The Head on the Statue of Liberty
9/18/68: 9   Puerto Rico's Centenary
11/2/68: 4   Why Puerto Ricans Urge Boycott of Poles
11/7/68: 9   Statehood Men Win in Puerto Rico
11/9/68: 4   Massive Mobilization to Protest Trial of 84
11/16/68: 4   15,000 Addicts
11/23/68: 4   A Change of Politics after the Elections?
11/30/68: 10   US Trusts' 'New Man' in Puerto Rico
12/7/68: 4   Facts Explode Myths Favoring Statehood
12/14/68: 4   Is Statehood Status Applicable to Nations?
12/21/68: 4   The MPI Anniversary
12/28/68: 4   Communists Assess Vote
1/4/69: 4   Policy Review Set by MPI; Eight Nationalists
                Freed
1/11/69: 4   Statehood's Champion As Seen by Patrons,
                Critics
1/18/69: 4   Ferré's Copper Plan
1/25/69: 4   Carmen Miranda is Dead, Was Teacher of
                Languages
2/1/69: 4   Ferré and the Copper Giveaway
2/8/69: 8   Modern Art by Puerto Rican Artists
2/15/69: 4   Betances Bought Freedom for Slave-Born Babes
3/1/69: 10   Brooklyn Library Discovers Puerto Ricans

Date   Title

Date	Title
3/8/69: 9	Yabucoa: A Town Marked for Death
3/15/69: 9	A Revolutionary Heroine
3/22/69: 9	N.Y. Memorial to Mark Ponce 1937 Massacre
3/29/69: 11	Uptown Project Named After Great Educator
4/5/69: 9	Will Badillo be New York's First Puerto Rican Mayor?
4/12/69: 9	Is Ferré Planning to Sell Puerto Rico's TV and Radio?
4/22/69: 9	All Puerto Ricans Honor Him
4/29/69: 10	Puerto Ricans Prepare for June 8 Parade
5/10/69: 9	Ferré's Police, FBI, Acting to Crush Independence Forces
5/17/69: 9	Puerto Rico's Poor Ousted to Build Hotels for the Rich
6/7/69: 10	Pro-Independencia in Sunday March Here
6/19/69: 6	*National Liberation*: Two Sides of Puerto Rican March
6/24/69: 9	San Juan Rotary Club Hears Racism's Voice
6/28/69: 11	Nationalist Party, Student Federation Denounces U. S. Conscription of Youth
7/8/69: 11	High School Students Map Fight on U. S. Army Draft
7/12/69: 11	2,000 Students Demand End of ROTC, Back Resisters
7/19/69: 9	Day for Joy or Mourning?
7/29/69: 11	A Party of Steadfast Heroes
8/5/69: 11	New Colonialism Increases Exploitation on the Island
8/9/69: 11	Why Washington Replaced Muñoz Marín with Luis Ferré
8/16/69: 9	Priests Fight for Free Speech
8/23/69: 11	Only Minority Seeks Statehood for P.R.
9/6/69: 10	Puerto Ricans Prepare for Albizu Campos Day
9/13/69: 9	Puerto Rican Painter Wins at Woodstock Art-Rock Fair
9/27/69: 6	*International*: First Congress of Puerto Rican Unions

Date	Title
10/4/69: 6	*Equality*: Racism and the Puerto Rican Parade
4/14/70: 10	Navy Scares a Caribbean Island
5/20/70: 10	U. S. Hotels Reject Demands
6/13/70: 10	Commencement to Honor Martyr
7/18/70: 10	Wages Cut Via Layoffs
7/28/70: 11	Latin American Writers Urge a Free Puerto Rico
8/15/70: 9	Puerto Rican Notes
9/12/70: 10	Memory of Albizu Campos Stirs Puerto Rico
9/19/70: 10	Secret Report Bares Puerto Witch Hunt
10/3/70: 10	A Careless Calendar of Puerto Rican History
10/24/70: 11	Growing Unemployment
12/19/70: 11	A Look at the Paper of Puerto Rican CP
2/13/71: 9	Puerto Rico Tenants Fight Phelps Dodge
2/27/71: 9	Events Set to Mark 1937 Ponce Massacre

The following are articles about Jesús Colón were published in *The Daily World*.

Date	Title
9/9/69: 11	Photograph of Jesús Colón and Rasheed Storey
9/9/69: 11	Storey, Colón Petitions Total 18,300
9/20/69: 4	Storey and Colón Offer a Radical Alternative
10/28/69: 4	Storey, Colón Hit Racist Call for Cops in Schools
11/4/69: 1	Photograph of Jesús Colón
11/6/69: 3	Election Return Results
5/16/74: 2	Jesús Colón Dies at the Age of 73
5/17/74: 2	Death of Jesús Colón Called Irreparable Loss
5/18/74: 2	Tribute to Jesús Colón Paid by Leaders of CP

VIII. Contents of *A Puerto Rican in New York and Other Sketches*

A Puerto Rican in New York and Other Sketches (New York: Masses and Mainstream, 1961; New York: International Publishers, 1982) is the only collection of writings published by Colón. Most of the sketches included in the book were previously published through his column *As I See It From Here* in *The Daily Worker*.

A Voice Through The Window
My First Literary Adventure
My First Strike
The Way to Learn
Stowaway
Easy Job, Good Wages
Two Men with but One Pair of Pants
On The Docks It Was Cold
I Heard A Man Crying
Kipling and I
How to Rent an Apartment
When You Don't Have Any Money
The Day My Father Got Lost
Hiawatha in Spanish
Name in Latin
A Hero in the Junk Truck
Maceo
The Story of Ana Roqué
Pisagua
Rivera Back in Mexico
Trujillo's Fair of Blood
Something To Read
The Origin of Latin American Dances (according to the Madison Avenue
    Boys)
Hollywood Rewrites History
Chinese Opera in Latin America
José
Sarah
Marcelino
Carmencita
The Lady Who Lived Near the Statue of a Man on a Horse
Little Things Are Big
The Mother, the Daughter, Myself and All of Us
Greetings from Washington
Because He Spoke in Spanish
Youth: The Palisades as a Backdrop
And Fuchik Looked on Confident
Wanted—A Statue
The Library Looks at the Puerto Ricans
On Singing in the Shower
How to Know the Puerto Ricans

Soap Box in the Swamps
My Private Hall of Fame
Books That Never Get Returned
Reading in the Bathtub
What Shall I Write About?
What D'Ya Read
The Visitor
Red Roses for Me
It Happened One Winter's Night
"I Made It"—"I Sold It"—"I Bought It"
Grandma, Please Don't Come!
She Actually Pinched Me!
Looking Just a Little Forward
For the Stay-at-Homes
If Instead of a Professor
A Puerto Rican in New York

IX. *The Way It Was: Puerto Ricans From Way Back*

Colón prepared an outline which listed over 240 pieces of writings that he wanted to include in a book entitled *The Way It Was: Puerto Ricans From Way Back*. The book manuscript was never completed and, as the many versions of the working book outline reveal, most of these pieces were to come from his many publications in newspapers and magazines during the more than five decades he lived in New York. Only a portion of the selections listed in the outline had not been published before. The ones listed below are those selections found among his papers, most of which are included in our volume.

Castor Oil: Simple or Compound?
Jesús Is Graduating Tonight
A Bright Child Asks a Question
He Couldn't Guess My Name
Nice to Have Friends in All Walks of Life
Dalmau
The Silent Contest
The Meanest Man in My Home Town
The *Fanguito* Is Still There

7: Jesús Colón, 1950s

List of Photographs

Photograph 1: Jesús Colón, circa 1940s

Photograph 2: Puerto Rican community demonstration, 1940s

Photograph 3: Liga Puertorriqueña e Hispana, Brooklyn Section.

Photograph 4: Vanguardia Puertorriqueña, Mother's Day Celebration, 1937

Photograph 5: Front page of *El Diario de Nueva York*, November 17, 1959

Photograph 6: Jesús Colón, 1960s

Photograph 7: Jesús Colón, 1950s

Photographic Credits:

Photographs 1, 3–7: The Jesús Colón Papers, Centro de Estudios Puertorriqueños, Hunter College; Benigno Giboyeaux, for the Estate of Jesús Colón and the Communist Party of the United States of America.

Photographs 2: Archivo Histórico, Departamento de Asuntos de la Comunidad Puertorriqueña en los Estados Unidos.

About the Editors

Edna Acosta-Belén is a Professor of Latin American and Caribbean Studies, and Women's Studies at the University at Albany, SUNY. She is also Director of the Center for Latin America and the Caribbean (CELAC). Her book publications include: *In the Shadow of the Giant: Colonialism, Migration, and Puerto Rican Culture* (forthcoming, 1993), *Researching Women in Latin America and the Caribbean* (with C. E. Bose, 1992), *The Puerto Rican Woman: Perspectives on Culture, History, and Society* (1979, 1986), *La mujer en la sociedad puertorriqueña* (1980) and *The Hispanic Experience in the United States* (with B. R. Sjostrom, 1986). She received her Ph.D. from Columbia University and has been a postdoctoral fellow at Princeton and Yale Universities.

Virginia Sánchez Korrol is an Associate Professor and Chair of the Department of Puerto Rican Studies at Brooklyn College. Her book publications include: *From Colonia to Community: The History of Puerto Ricans in New York City* (1983, 1993) and *The Puerto Rican Struggle: Essays on Survival in the U. S.* (with C. Rodríguez and J. O. Alers, 1980, 1984). She is the first President of the Puerto Rican Studies Association (PRSA) and was appointed by the New York State Regents and the Commissioner of Education to the Social Studies Curriculum and Assessment Committee. She was also a member of the New York State Ibero-American Heritage Curriculum Project Advisory and Editorial Board. Her Ph.D. is from SUNY-Stony Brook.